My Peace
I Give You

"A sensitive and poignant effort to offer the gift of healing to some of the most wounded people of our time, with the aid of the wisdom of the great saints. A book that is both moving and useful."

Rev. James Martin, S.J.
Author of *Between Heaven and Mirth*

"Dawn Eden tackles this most difficult of issues with tenderness and grace. She mixes practical advice with inspiration from the lives of the saints, and in doing so reminds us that there are no wounds so deep that the Lord cannot heal them."

Jennifer Fulwiler
Blogger at *ConversionDiary.com*

"*My Peace I Give You* is a modern-day *Confessions* and is intended to touch the heart of anyone who suffered from any kind of harm or loss in childhood or anyone sensitive enough to say that life sometimes hurts. It is honest, sincere, and hopeful, weaving one's hurts and losses into the complete and comprehensive Good News of Jesus Christ. This is the kind of theology that is accessible to the human heart. I hope you will find here as much grace as I did. Thank you, Dawn."

Rev. Gregory John Mansour
Bishop of the Eparchy of Saint Maron of Brooklyn

"A powerful and poignant voice formulating in words the unspoken cry of the heart from those who have been shamefully abused and violated. Dawn Eden—a victim herself—shows readers that there is healing not in repression or misplaced self-blame, but in hiding in the wounds of Christ."

Alice von Hildebrand
Author of *The Privilege of Being a Woman*

"Filled with wisdom and compassion, *My Peace I Give You* is Dawn Eden's gift to victims of childhood sexual abuse and anyone struggling with hurts inflicted by others. She offers inspiration from saints who were themselves abused but found healing in Christ, through whose wounds we too can be healed."

Rev. R. Scott Hurd
Author of *Forgiveness: A Catholic Approach*

"Dawn has done a great service for the twenty-first-century Church on this most difficult topic. She is honest without being tawdry. Scholarly without being aloof. Compassionate without being pandering. Devout without being being black and white. Everybody needs to read this."

Barbara Nicolosi Harrington
Executive Director
The Galileo Forum and Studio at Azusa Pacific University

My Peace
I Give You

Healing Sexual Wounds with the Help of the Saints

Dawn Eden

ave maria press AᴹᵖP notre dame, indiana

Nihil Obstat: Reverend Carter H. Griffin, S.T.D.
                    Censor Deputatus

Imprimatur: His Eminence Donald Cardinal Wuerl
                    Archbishop of Washington
                    Given at Washington, District of Columbia, on
                    14 December 2011.

Founded in 1865, Ave Maria Press is a ministry of the United States Province of Holy Cross.

www.avemariapress.com

ISBN-10 1-59471-290-5   ISBN-13 978-1-59471-290-6

Cover photography © Rachel DelaGardelle from stock.xchng.com.

Cover and text design by Andy Wagoner.

Printed and bound in the United States of America.

Library of Congress Cataloging-in-Publication Data is available.

To Fr. Daniel A. Lord, S.J.
(1888–1955),
who, in a time of depression, said to his Lord,
"It may well be that I shall find you in the depths
before I shall find you upon the heights";
whose witness of courage and love
in the face of terminal illness
fueled my desire to write this book;
who was in my mind and heart
at every moment as I wrote;
and whose cause for sainthood I hope to postulate,
this book is gratefully dedicated.

Contents

Foreword

I have waited years for this book. As a psychologist and a consecrated religious, I am sobered and sorrowed by the sheer number of adults whose lives are marked by the shadow of sexual abuse. This failure to protect a child's innocence reverberates throughout a victim's entire life. In my knowledge, a victim of sexual abuse often struggles, even as an adult, to conquer the relentless temptations of self-condemnation. In the pages that follow, readers find an alternative to self-loathing; they find hope and a cause for joy. *My Peace I Give You* is an inspired work that provides a map toward the integrated healing of the mind, body, emotions, and soul of those who have suffered the shattering effects of sexual abuse either directly or indirectly.

Like a generous and gracious host, Dawn Eden freely shares herself and her friends as she introduces us to well-known and lesser-known saints all the while weaving her personal story throughout. You may be amazed and relieved to find that among those whom the Church assures us are closest to the Heart of Jesus are adults wounded and healed; adults whose wounds became the source of the greatness of their love because it opened the door to a definitive transformation in Jesus Christ; and saints who now rejoice in the words of the Easter liturgy: "Oh, happy fault!" They have lived firsthand the experience of the life-changing power of the love of God and know the truth of Jesus' words: "My grace is sufficient for you, for my power is made perfect in weakness."

As I journeyed with the saints through these pages, I was reminded of a little poem that possesses a riveting

image of Jesus as he descends to the dead on the first Holy
Saturday. Our victorious Lord is received by the patri-
archs and prophets, Adam and Eve, and all who have died
under the law still marked by the wounds of his Passion.
Those same wounds are "five crimson stars." Allow me
to share a few lines:

> And there He was
>> splendid as the morning sun and fair
>> as only God is fair.
> And they, confused with joy,
>> knelt to adore
>> seeing that He wore
>> five crimson stars
>> He never had before.[1]

This image captures something of the beauty of the
healing that is promised to each of us in Christ Jesus.
Indeed, we are promised healing, but we may be surprised
to find that the gift of wholeness will be routed in and
through our wounds. This, of course, should come as no
surprise at all, for the way to greatness for all Christians is
in the imitation of Our Lord and Savior, Jesus Christ. It is
the hallmark of Christian spirituality that "by his wounds
we are healed (Is 53:5 NIV)." It is also one of the themes
included in this powerfully moving and hope-filled book.

Dawn Eden reveals this truth by explaining that in
experiencing the love of God, one is freed to love oneself
deeply and well, and then others. It is my hope that this
book may become a resource readily available in churches,
schools, counseling centers, young adult ministries, libraries, and hospitals. Through it, may many whose human
dignity has been offended come to know their beauty in
the eyes of God, and learn to sing in joy of his love and

mercy. I pray that this book will be an instrument of grace and instruction.

Mother Agnes Mary Donovan, S.V.

Sisters of Life

Acknowledgments

Thanks go first to homeschool educator Julia Fogassy, as it was at her home in December 2010 that I got the idea to write a book like this upon discovering Blessed Laura Vicuña's story in Ann Ball's *Modern Saints: Their Lives and Faces*. A few weeks later, Ave Maria Press assistant editor Kristi McDonald contacted me to introduce herself. The enthusiasm that she and editorial director Bob Hamma showed for the concept of *My Peace I Give You* gave me the encouragement I needed to develop it further. My sincerest gratitude goes out to them and everyone at Ave Maria Press. Many thanks as well to my literary agent, Wes Yoder, and everyone at the Ambassador Agency.

I was extraordinarily blessed to have many experts and friends provide feedback during the writing process, including Fr. Joseph Alobaidi, O.P.; Drusilla Barron; Fr. Phil Bloom; Dr. Carole Burnett; Judit Crow; Sarah Dickerson; William Doino Jr.; Kevin Doyle; Fr. Paul Dressler, O.F.M.; Fr. Scott Hurd; Fr. John Baptist Ku, O.P.; Br. John Luth, M.I.C.; Fr. James Martin, S.J.; Martha McNeill; Grace Mortemore; Fr. Bernard Mulcahy, O.P.; Terry Nelson; Colin O'Brien; Deanna Olsen; Éric Plante; Timothy Post; Fr. Sean Raftis; and Magdalen Ross. Other invaluable aid came from Maria Krzemińska, who donated her talents to translate materials on Blessed Karolina, and from the Sisters of Charity of Quebec, who showed me kind hospitality while I wrote. Many more friends provided prayers and moral support. Thanks to all—you know who you are—and especially to Sr. Jane Dominic Laurel, O.P., and Janet Rosen.

My deepest gratitude goes to Fr. Gabriel O'Donnell, O.P., vice president and academic dean of Dominican House of Studies, for showing faith in me when I approached him seeking to study theology. Thanks as well to all my professors not yet mentioned, especially Fr. John Corbett, O.P., and Fr. John Langlois, O.P., and to my schoolmates.

Thanks beyond words to all my family, especially for their prayers.

In memoriam: Fr. Francis Canavan, S.J.; Sr. Geraldine Calabrese, M.P.F.; Jeffry Hendrix; Stephanie Nooney; Eleanor Ruder; and Archbishop Pietro Sambi.

Finally, I would like to thank Janet E. Smith, for reminding me that it is better to light a single candle than to curse the darkness.

Introduction

This book has been on my heart for a long time. It comes from the desire to bring the joy of communion to those living with the spiritually isolating effects of childhood sexual abuse.

Through the communion I have discovered, which is the Communion of Saints, my spirit has been transformed and continues to be transformed—gaining healing, strength, and comfort beyond what I ever thought possible. I pray that the following stories of saints' personal sufferings and triumphs will guide you to this same experience of joyful transformation in Christ.

But perhaps you are wondering what the saints could possibly have to do with healing from childhood wounds, especially those wounds that are most hurtful and least talked about. Explaining that connection requires me to revisit a time when my life did not have so much light.

■ ■ ■

I can still remember the first time I ever read a verse of the Gospel—perhaps because of the novelty of seeing something from the "other" Bible (my family was Jewish), but most likely because it made me cry.

The verse appeared at the end of Hans Christian Andersen's fairy tale "The Snow Queen," after Gerda's innocent love rescues Kai from the Snow Queen's icy clutches. The girl and boy joyfully return to Grandmother's home, just as Grandmother is reading Jesus' words in Matthew 18:3: "Unless you turn and become like children, you will never enter the kingdom of heaven."

Reading those words filled me with an inexpressible feeling of longing, mingled with loss. I wanted with all my heart to be a joyful, innocent child. Instead, I felt as though my childhood had already vanished into thin air. It had disappeared before I had even realized it existed.

I kept looking at the page, but my gaze lost its focus as I became absorbed in thought. My throat contracted, and tears welled up. How could this be? Here I was, weeping inconsolably for my lost childhood—and I was only seven years old.

Now I know. The tears came because, even at that young age, I had suffered sexual abuse. What's more, for the previous two years, since my parents had split up and my mother gained custody, I had been living in an environment I would now consider to be sexually porous. I don't recall any clear boundaries; I was not well shielded from adults' nudity, substance abuse, dirty jokes, sex talk, and swearing.

Like many victims of sexual abuse, I identify with the words of the messenger in Job 1:15: "I alone have escaped to tell you." As far as I know, there is no other living person who admits to witnessing the evils that were done to me.[1] Certainly, my mother recalls things very differently than I do. When I told her of the incidents I planned to relate in this book, she denied several of them, including that her home was a "sexually porous environment" during my childhood.[2]

Placing myself back in the mind of that little girl who loved Andersen's fairy tales, I realize that, as dazzling as those stories were to my young imagination, nothing in them seemed more wondrous—or more out of reach—than the pure and uncomplicated childhood of Gerda and

Kai, surrounded by the love of their grandmother and the love of God.

■ ■ ■

By the time I was thirty-one, when I received the gift of faith in Christ, I understood more clearly how the Lord's words in Matthew's gospel referred to spiritual and not literal childhood. A few years after that, as my faith drew me into the Catholic Church, I discovered that the *Catechism* links this spiritual childhood with being "born from above" (Jn 3:7)—the new life of grace that begins with baptism.

Learning about the ongoing aid that grace provides in the moral life was encouraging, helping me be patient with myself as I began to "walk the walk" of a faithful Christian. As time went by, however, my initial confidence began to erode. My greatest desire was to have the blessing Jesus promises to the "pure in heart, . . . for they shall see God" (Mt 5:8). Yet, even when I was doing everything I could to live in purity, I was unable to *feel* pure. I felt stained—because of what adults had done to me, or had bid me do, when I was a helpless child.

On an intellectual level, I knew there was nothing for me to be ashamed of. No child is responsible for what an adult does to her, or induces her to do. The sin of abuse belongs to the abusers, not their victims. Children depend on adults and have to trust them in order to survive. It is adults' responsibility to show children what is good, and it is in children's very nature to accept what adults call "good" as being truly good. One cannot speak of "consent" in such an unequal relationship.

As I began to read more about what Christians believe, I found that the Church Fathers and Doctors ("Doctor" being a title given to saints of the highest wisdom) said many powerful things in defense of victims of sexual abuse. St. Augustine, writing about the virgin martyrs of the early Church, lashed out at pagans who claimed that virgins who had been raped were no longer virgins: "What sane man can suppose that, if his body be seized and forcibly made use of to satisfy the lust of another, he thereby loses his purity?"[3]

Although I was aware of these things, try as I might I was unable to internalize the knowledge that I was innocent of what had been done to me. Instead, I felt like there was a black mark on my childhood, a blotch of indelible ink. The more I tried to cover up this feeling by repressing the bad memories, the more the pain, loss, and shame threatened to seep into every corner of my adult life.

■ ■ ■

After I entered the Catholic Church in 2006, my journey toward healing began in earnest. I learned an ancient prayer that opened me up to a new understanding of the workings of grace. It is called the *Anima Christi* ("Soul of Christ") and begins with these words:

> Soul of Christ, sanctify me
> Body of Christ, save me
> Blood of Christ, inebriate me
> Water from Christ's side, wash me
> Passion of Christ, strengthen me
> O good Jesus, hear me
> Within Thy wounds hide me
> Suffer me not to be separated from Thee . . .[4]

Do you notice how the prayer's perspective shifts? It goes from asking Christ to be within you to asking that you may be within him. More than that, where in Christ are you asking to be sheltered? Within his *wounds*.

Until I began to reflect upon that prayer, my faith life was entangled in a forest of questions: How could I believe in God's protective love, when my own family failed to protect me? How could I be a child to God when I never had a real childhood? How could I be pure when I never knew purity?

Those questions seemed pressing and deep, but in reality they were dead ends, keeping me confined in the solitude of self. The *Anima Christi*'s intense symbolism inspired me to ask questions that would lead me out of that prison—questions like, How can Christ's Passion strengthen me? What does it mean to have him live in me, and for me to live in him? But by far the most important question to emerge from reflecting upon that prayer was, How can Jesus' wounds draw me closer to him? The answer, unfolding gradually over the course of the next few years, would change the way I understood my own wounds.

■ ■ ■

The disciples were convinced of the Resurrection only when Christ showed them his wounded hands, feet, and—for the doubting Thomas—his side.

In paintings of the risen Christ, the Sacred Heart is often depicted aflame with fiery rays. We see this most dramatically in the Divine Mercy image, based on St. Faustina Kowalska's vision, in which Jesus' heart shines forth brilliant streams of white and red light. I picture Jesus' wounds as they appear in those images, radiating grace—a "glowing furnace" of love, as one prayer puts it.[5] When praying, "Within your wounds, hide me," I am asking to be hidden in those wounds, which are now glorified. I want to be surrounded and protected by their overflowing graces, the healing rays that extend to the ends of the earth.

Over time, as that image of the loving and merciful light streaming from Jesus' wounds deepened its hold on my consciousness, I began to re-examine the times in my past when I had doubted God's mercy. That in turn led to a conversation with God that I had been putting off for a long time—asking how I could embody his mercy toward those I found hardest to forgive.

■ ■ ■

New Catholics are eager to read stories about the saints, and I was no exception. But when I delved into the lives of those who had suffered the most—the early Roman martyrs—it gave me a bad case of TMI: Too Much Information. The ancient authors' graphic descriptions of torture were more than I could handle.

That same discomfort surfaces when I read about people who suffered childhood abuse—even when I know their stories have a happy ending. In fact, because my own experiences have left me with post-traumatic stress disorder, I have to be cautious about my media consumption, as certain emotional triggers can cause me to flash back to the abuse. Knowing this makes me very sensitive to others who likewise, although wanting to know they are not alone in their experience, do not wish to relive their trauma. So, as I share in this book about my own journey and those of the saints, I will be careful to avoid details beyond those needed to make the stories meaningful and real.

There are some topics that will not be shared here, not because they are unimportant, but because they are beyond my field of expertise. For example, this book is not intended for those who are currently in a sexually abusive relationship or need advice on bringing an abuser to justice, although some of the organizations listed among the resources at the back of this book may be helpful.

In addition, although I share my fellow Catholics' grief and anger over those who have betrayed their sacred office, I will not focus on the scandal of abuse committed by clergy. The reason for this is not out of any desire to diminish the very real and often devastating experiences of those who have suffered such abuse. I fervently hope this book will help them and those who minister to them. However, I am taking a more general perspective, based on my personal experience as part of a large population whose needs are not currently being met. By far the largest category of childhood sexual-abuse perpetrators are family members, who are responsible for about one-third to one-half of cases. After that (in descending order) come family friends, neighbors, acquaintances, and strangers; only a small percentage of cases are committed by clergy. Given how many American adults report having been sexually abused as children—about 1 in 4 women and 1 in 6 men, according to the Centers for Disease Control—such painful memories afflict at least one person in every pew in every parish.[6] If you are among those victims,[7] I want you to know you are not alone, you are not forgotten, and you have more friends in heaven than you realize.

■ ■ ■

Admitting to having been abused is more than I was able to do when I was writing my first book, *The Thrill of the Chaste*, which was published in December 2006. The topic of that book—on learning how to live joyfully while saving sex for marriage—required sharing a great deal about my past. However, I had no vocabulary at that time to describe what had been done to me as a child. The memories were there, to be sure, but they were tied up in a confusing knot of emotions.

It was not until the following year that a therapist convinced me that I had to come to terms with that part of my life, including taking an honest look at the impact my past experiences had on my present relationships with those close to me. For many who have been abused in the home, recognizing what was done to them and beginning the healing process requires breaking their emotional dependence upon the person who perpetrated the abuse. Like hostages who have "Stockholm syndrome," such victims, having no one else to whom they could turn, developed an unhealthy attachment to their abuser.[8] Although my situation was different in that those who abused me did not live in my home, I came to realize that I needed to likewise break my emotional dependence upon the person I had most hoped would protect me: my mother.

One evening in July 2006, over dinner with my mother and stepfather at a Chinese restaurant, I finally asked my mother some questions. With her honest answers, a fuller picture of what had happened began to take shape.

My questions centered upon the first abuse I could remember. It was different from other harmful events from my childhood in that it took place outside the home, at the temple where my mother, who had recently separated from my father, took my sister and me on Friday nights for Shabbat (the Jewish Sabbath). As a five-year-old, I found the worship service boring, so my mother let me hang out in the temple's library until it was over. The only other person around was Al, the temple's janitor, age seventy-three.

After at least two such Shabbats, maybe more, I recall walking with my mother on a Saturday afternoon outside the apartment complex where we lived, and saying to her, "Al and I have a secret and I'm not supposed to tell you."

My mother of course insisted I tell her. I felt simultaneously stupid and afraid—stupid for opening my big mouth and afraid of what Mom would do when she found out.

"Well," I began—and here I have to pause as I write, because, even though the abuse took place more than thirty-five years ago, it is still painful to describe. It is painful not so much because of what Al did to me, but rather because of the embarrassment and shame I remember feeling at my mother's reaction, which my young mind interpreted as being full of disappointment and anger.

"Al has me play a game with him," I said. "He sucks my tongue, and then he has me suck his tongue."

Mom turned to me sharply. "What else does he do?" she demanded.

"Um . . ." Now I'm really sunk, I thought. "He puts his hand on my leg—on my thigh."

I remember my Mom's response as being loud and abrupt. She had gone to acting school, and her voice was overpowering when she let it project. "He *feels* you *up*?" she exclaimed.

That expression was new to my young mind. "I—I guess so."

"How could you let him do that?"

"I didn't mean to! It was *his* idea."

As she persisted in questioning me, shame surged up like a smothering wave. "I didn't know," I sputtered. "I mean, I knew, but . . ."

"If you knew it was wrong, how could you let it happen?"

I couldn't give an acceptable answer. It is hard to respond to that kind of question at any age, and impossible when you are just entering first grade.

There was more to the story, none of it pleasant. My mother brought the matter to the attention of the rabbi— Al's boss. The rabbi questioned Al, who denied everything. After feeling that, in my mother's eyes, I was a girl who "let" an old man do dirty things to her, I was now, in the rabbi's eyes, a liar.* Not wanting to breathe a word of the incident to my father—for fear that he, too, would suggest I was to blame—I left it to my mother to tell him.

All those things I could remember without any help as I had dinner with my mother that evening in 2006, more than thirty years later. What I wanted to know from her was why she didn't tell my father. At my therapist's suggestion, I had recently tried to discuss it with Dad and was surprised when he insisted he had never been told about it.

---

* It is only fair to acknowledge the influence of the era on my mother and the rabbi's reactions. Pedophilia was far less understood in the early 1970s than it is today, and little was done to stop or prevent it. In 2006, after I asked my mother about her memory of the Al episode, she wrote to the rabbi to seek his recollection. He responded with deep regret: "I believe that neither you nor I knew how to handle this situation in the mid-1970s and would have dealt with it much differently if we confronted it today."

I remember her answer as being straightforward and disarmingly direct: "I didn't tell him, because it would have affected custody."*

Of course. At the time I was molested, my parents had not yet divorced, and there was still a chance for my father to contest my mother's request for sole custody of my sister and me.

The custody comment subtly told me that it was more important to my mother for me to be "hers" than for me to be safe. She insisted she did not mean it that way, but, to me, it was a revelation: I was able to understand for the first time why it was so hard for me to find my own identity apart from her. Children find their identity through belonging. In experiencing the love and security of belonging to their family, they come to learn that they and all their family belong to God. There is an order to this belonging—parents protect children, and children obey parents—yet there is equality in that the belonging is based on mutual giving. Family members belong to one another. Even God belongs to us in this way, as it says in Song of Songs: "I am my beloved's and my beloved is mine" (6:3).

It is through our belonging that we understand how we are related to one another, and it is through these relations that we understand our individuality. I am my mother's daughter, therefore I am not my mother; I am my own person.

As a child in my mother's home, I did not experience this true belonging. As I look back from my perspective

* This is my own personal recollection of my mother's reply. In writing this book, I reminded her of this conversation and she denied having said such a thing. My father says that, had he been informed of Al's abusing me, he would indeed have sought custody of my sister and me.

today, the only belonging I can remember was the experience of belonging to my mother as a *possession*. It is no wonder, then, that I grew up without knowing who I was. Not understanding what it meant to belong to a family, I could not yet understand what it meant to belong to God.

■ ■ ■

One of the most beautiful and mysterious verses in the Bible contains God's words to Paul, after the saint begged the Lord to heal him of something that was causing him pain: "My grace is sufficient for you, for my power is made perfect in weakness"(2 Cor 12:9). That same power is what we see when we contemplate the resurrected Lord, as the wound he received to his Sacred Heart becomes a fountain of life. If we accept the overflowing grace he offers us, the wounds we received in our weakness bear witness to the strength we receive from the One who overcame death.

The people who are truly weakest are often those who put forth a false front of impenetrability. They live in fear that their imperfections will be discovered, like gods of iron with feet of clay. I see this now in my mother, who has worked desperately to keep up the image of being a "perfect mom." Even now, I feel, her resistance to my memories of abuse—the worst of which I remember being perpetrated in her presence by one of her boyfriends—is fueled by fear of vulnerability.

Over time I have come to realize it was all she could do to admit the harmful events occurred—which, to her credit, she did. It was not fair of me to expect her to provide me the emotional closure I sought, because she was not strong enough. She was wounded too, but I suspect she thought the only way she could survive was to deny having any chinks in her armor. I should have compassion on her, because I used to close myself off like that—and sometimes still do.

A common response to pain is to put up emotional walls and hide. The first thing I do when sensing a flash-back coming on is to dash to a place where no one can see me cry. But the times I am closest to being whole are, paradoxically, the times when I can admit, like songwriter Leonard Cohen, that "there is a crack, a crack in every-thing; that's how the light gets in."

Here is where the saints have something to show us. We tend to think of the saints in heaven as being perfect, which they are, but it would be more descriptive to say they have been *perfected*. Likewise, we think of the saints as being pure, which they also are, but it would be truer to say they have been *purified*. The prophet Malachi spoke of this purification when he described the Messiah as "like a refiner's fire," adding that "he will purify the sons of Levi and refine them like gold and silver, till they present right offerings to the Lord" (3:2–3).

But it is not just the "sons of Levi"—that is, those called to official religious duties—who present offerings to the Lord. It is me and you and everyone, insomuch as I received my soul as a gift from God and will one day be called to return everything I am to God. The saints are the ones who, during the course of their lives, allowed God to perfect and purify them so that they could return a gift even more beautiful than the one they first received.

The language of "purification" does not apply to Mary, who was pure from her conception. What we can say is that, from her "yes" at the Annunciation to the end of her earthly life, she let herself be progressively formed into a greater likeness of her Son. She underwent her spiritual configuration in the same way all the saints are conformed to the image of Christ—through a self-gift completed by suffering. In this offering, as Fulton J. Sheen wrote, "the dross of pain [is] transmuted into the gold of sacrifice by the alchemy of love."[9]

Like her Son, Mary had a wounded heart—only her wound was the kind that cannot be seen (Lk 2:35). Instead of letting her wound fester, she responded to it by opening her heart to be the Mother of the entire Church (Jn. 19:26). We see her on the Miraculous Medal the way she appeared to St. Catherine Labouré, her open hands ready to shower down graces on all who request them. She whose soul was unblemished let her heart bear the crack where the light got in.

What the saints taught me, and are still teaching me, is what I want to share with you in this book. I think of it as a great hidden truth, although it is not elite or special knowledge. Neither is it really hidden, except in the sense of being hidden in plain sight; it unfolds throughout the Bible (especially the letters of St. Paul) as well as the *Catechism*. It only seems hidden because it is so beautiful that once you begin to realize its importance, you want to reveal it to the whole world: All suffering contains within it the opportunity to become more like the One who suffered on the Cross.

No matter what evil was done to us, if we, like the saints, offer our hearts to God, he will accept us as we are, with all our past experiences. Your heart right now contains all the raw material he needs to mold it so that, with his grace working over the course of time, it may become like his. This is true no matter how damaged you may feel. So long as our hearts long for union with Jesus' Sacred Heart, our feelings about ourselves will not prevent such union, because God's love is stronger than feelings. It is a *presence*.

This loving presence is what the saints now enjoy, and what they want to bring to us, through their example and prayers. The stories of their lives—how they suffered, and how they emerged from their sufferings into greater holiness—show that God not only wants to heal our wounds: if we let him, he will heal us *through* our wounds, making everything we have endured serve to draw us nearer to him in love.

■ ■ ■

As I began to study the saints, I was not surprised to learn that among those whom the Church has formally declared to be in heaven were people who were sexually abused as youths. The stories of the early martyrs are familiar enough; so too is that of Maria Goretti, who was fatally stabbed while resisting sexual assault. What surprised me was the sheer number of saints who experienced such abuse—there were many more than I had imagined— and how relevant their stories were to people living in the present day. In the United States of the twenty-first century, children may not know what it is like to be at the mercy of a pagan emperor, but many know what it is like to be at the mercy of their mother's violent, alcoholic live-in lover, as was Blessed Laura Vicuña. They are not thrown to the lions, but many are thrown into a sexually invasive home environment, as was St. Thomas Aquinas. They may not know the breaking wheel, but many have their young hearts broken, like Blessed Margaret of Castello, whose parents abandoned her because she was blind and physically deformed.

Another surprise was discovering how human the saints were in their reactions to abuse. They weren't all sweetness and light. It was a guilty pleasure to read how the young Bernardine of Siena reacted when a rich man propositioned him while he was playing in a field with schoolmates. According to an early biographer, the little saint to be promptly whopped the man upside the head. (While he may very well have been justified, perhaps this is an apt moment to recall the old saying—often quoted by Dorothy Day—that one could go to hell imitating the imperfections of the saints.)

In researching this book, I also learned, through a conversation with an investigating judge for the Vatican Congregation for the Causes of Saints, that St. Augustine's teaching on virgin martyrs remains the doctrine of the Church. A virgin who was raped before being martyred is still considered a martyr of chastity. In fact, the official said, there is a twentieth-century martyr of chastity, a teenage girl beatified by Pope John Paul II, whose physical intactness could not be positively ascertained after her martyrdom, owing to decomposition.

When the official told me the girl's name, I was shocked, because popular accounts of her martyrdom claim she was not violated—implying that, if she had been violated, she would not be a saint. He, however, being well acquainted with the facts of the case, insisted the girl in question—a virgin who lived a holy life—was declared a martyr of chastity purely because of evidence she *resisted* rape. Whether the rape attempt was completed is something we will never know. Chapter 8 reveals the identity of this saint, a true patron for victims of childhood sexual abuse.

∎ ∎ ∎

About that conversation with God that I mentioned, the one where I asked him how to embody his mercy toward those I found hardest to forgive: if the truth be told, that was not a one-time discussion. This process of forgiveness is ongoing, and I am not just querying God one on one. I am also seeking his guidance through his saints—those you will meet in this book—and listening to the answers they give through the examples of their lives.

Pope Benedict XVI observes that man needs to be saved from the sorrow and bitterness that cause him to forsake God. For this liberation to take effect, "transformation from within is necessary, some foothold of goodness, a beginning from which to start out in order to change evil into good, hatred into love, revenge into forgiveness."[10] I invite you to join me in discovering this "foothold of goodness" through the stories of holy people who, having experienced some of the greatest sorrows that the world could offer, were yet able to turn their eyes toward heaven and be saved.

CHAPTER 1

The Love We Forget

Discovering the Father— with St. Ignatius Loyola and St. Josephine Bakhita

> Little Kai was blue—indeed, almost black— from the cold; but he did not feel it, for the Snow Queen had kissed all feeling of coldness out of him, and his heart had almost turned into a lump of ice. He sat arranging and rearranging pieces of ice into patterns. . . . He wanted to put the pieces of ice together in such a way that they formed a certain word, but he could not remember exactly what that word was. The word that he could not remember was "eternity."
>
> —Hans Christian Andersen
> "The Snow Queen"

When St. Ignatius of Loyola underwent a dramatic spiritual conversion in 1521 at the age of thirty, there were many things in his past that he would have liked to forget. His mother had died when he was just a baby, and soon afterward his father had sent him away from the family home, to be raised by a wet nurse. Although he grew to feel at home in his nurse's family, the experiences of loss and upheaval at such a young age likely took an emotional toll on the saint.

What we know for certain is that Ignatius bore deep regrets for things he had brought upon himself. He would later say that, before he was awakened to the love of Christ, he was "enthralled by the vanities of the world" and especially the military life, where he "seemed led by a strong and empty desire of gaining for himself a great name."[1] We also have his friends' account that he was "reckless" with games, women, and brawls.

Years later, St. Ignatius wrote his Spiritual Exercises, which over time would help millions discover God's call in their lives. Toward the end of the regimen of meditations, he included a prayer for perfect charity—the virtue that unites us most fully in love to God and one another. In the first line of this prayer, known as the *Suscipe* (after its first word in Latin), we find an important clue to the nature of Ignatius's own spiritual journey:

> Take, O Lord, and receive all my liberty, my memory, my understanding, and my whole will. Thou hast given me all that I am and all that I possess; I surrender it all to thee that thou mayest dispose of it according to thy will. Give me only thy love and thy grace; with these I will be content and will have no more to desire.[2]

The first thing Ignatius offers God is his liberty. Wanting to live for God instead of for himself, Ignatius gives up his freedom to act, so that he might say with St. Paul, "I have been crucified with Christ; it is no longer I who live, but Christ who lives in me" (Gal 2:20).

Then comes the aspect of the *Suscipe* prayer that is perhaps the most striking. Having given his freedom, Ignatius seeks to give God his mind and heart. What is the first part of his inner self that he offers? It is his *memory*.

In Ignatius's understanding of the human mind, the concept of memory refers to more than just particular memories. Memory includes everything that had entered into his consciousness to make him who he was—whether or not he could actually remember it. It forms the foundation of his present identity, including his hopes for his future.

This is an ancient way of understanding memory, dating back at least to St. Augustine, and it makes particular sense for one who has survived trauma—as Ignatius had, having been wounded during his military days. Often in trauma survivors (and this holds regardless of whether the trauma was the result of sexual abuse or military combat) the brain attempts to protect itself by consigning painful swaths of the past to areas where memory's tendrils cannot reach them. Yet the memories of traumatic events, whether present to us or not, remain part of us.

That is why there is something very beautiful about St. Ignatius offering his memory to God. The saint acknowledges there are things he cannot change—the events of his past—and at the same time displays the bold hope that his Maker will accept him *as he is now*, with everything he did and everything that was done to him. Such is true abandonment to divine providence—joyfully accepting in your own life the truth encapsulated in the old proverb, "God writes straight with crooked lines."

The fathers of the Second Vatican Council, writing of Christ's Passion, said that "the Holy Spirit in a manner known only to God offers to every man the possibility of being associated with this paschal mystery."[3] Ignatius discovered in his own life that the Holy Spirit was able to use all the experiences that had shaped him—all the traumas he endured, as well as the mistakes he made along the way—to bring him to the love of Christ.

Pope John Paul II once reflected, "I have often stopped to look at the long queues of pilgrims waiting patiently to go through the Holy Door. In each of them I tried to imagine the story of a life, made up of joys, worries, sufferings; the story of someone whom Christ had met and who, in dialogue with him, was setting out again on a journey of hope."[4]

This "journey of hope" was the journey of Ignatius, who was nicknamed "the Pilgrim," and it becomes ours as we pray his *Suscipe*. In dialogue with the Risen One, we set out on a journey of hope, believing with St. Paul that, having been crucified with Christ, "the life I now live in the flesh I live by faith in the Son of God, who loved me and gave himself for me" (Gal 2:20).

Memory does not have to be, nor should it be, the enemy. Rather, as Pope Benedict XVI has written, "Memory and hope are inseparable. To poison the past does not give hope: it destroys its emotional foundations."[5]

■ ■ ■

In every childhood, even the most troubled, there are moments of joy, however fleeting—the joy of wonder. A certain African saint never forgot the sense of awe she experienced as a child: "Seeing the sun, the moon and the stars, I said to myself: Who could be the Master of these beautiful things? And I felt a great desire to see him, to know him and to pay him homage."[6]

It is a remarkable testimony to grace that this saint could still recall that moment of awe years later. Not long after she experienced it, she was traumatized so deeply that she forgot her own name.

■ ■ ■

I became interested in the life of St. Josephine Bakhita, the first-ever canonized saint to be born in Sudan, after Pope Benedict praised her as "a saint of our time" who can help us understand what it means to have a real encounter with God for the first time.[7] Reading her story, I was struck by how many aspects of the saint's experience are as familiar to abuse victims in modern-day America as they were to slaves in nineteenth-century Africa.

The girl who would become known as Bakhita was born around 1869 (she was never certain of the date). During the first several years of her life, she enjoyed the security of a large and loving family. She had three sisters, including a twin, and three brothers; her father was a landowner, and her uncle was the head of the village where they lived. As she would recall when telling her story years later, she was "as happy as could be, and didn't know the meaning of sorrow."[8]

All that changed when slave raiders began to make incursions into the area where the family lived, a village in the Darfur region. One morning when Bakhita was seven, she was out gathering herbs with an adolescent female friend when "all of a sudden two ugly armed strangers emerged from a hedge."[9] The thugs told the friend to move along. As soon as she was out of sight, they snatched Bakhita—one holding a knife at her side, the other pushing her forward with a gun to her back.

Recounting her kidnapping, Bakhita highlighted the fact that she was too frightened to speak: "I was petrified with fear, my eyes staring, trembling from head to foot. I tried to scream, but there was a lump in my throat: I couldn't speak or cry out."[10] One of the kidnappers asked her name, but she was unable to form an answer.

Bakhita's story brings back memories of my own nightmares. Like many survivors of childhood sexual abuse (as well as others who suffer from post-traumatic stress disorder), I have experienced terrifying dreams in which I relive feelings of helplessness. In real life, as an abused child, I could not speak up for myself and had no one who would speak for me. In dreams, I relive this experience when, chased by attackers, I try to scream and am unable to make a sound. Bakhita truly endured, in every sense, the voicelessness of the victim. And, as we shall see, she was not without nightmares.

The captors ordered the terrified little girl to call herself Bakhita, which meant "Lucky." It was then that, as a result of the extreme fear and upheaval she endured, she forgot the name her parents gave her. Bakhita effectively underwent, in dramatic form, an experience psychologists say is shared by many victims of childhood sexual abuse—loss of personal identity:

> The development of a sense of self is thought to be one of the earliest developmental tasks of the infant and young child, typically unfolding in the context of early relationships. How a child is treated (or maltreated) early in life influences his or her growing self-awareness. As a result, severe child maltreatment—including early and sustained sexual abuse—may interfere with the child's development of a sense of self.[11]

What is meant here by a "sense of self" includes an understanding of boundaries—where the other person ends and you begin. Childhood sexual abuse is a transgression upon the child's personal sphere. Beyond that insight, however, psychologists have a hard time explaining what proper self-identity actually entails. The best they can do is to explain it negatively: the individual finds himself by finding that he is not another person. The problem with such a definition is that it disregards the reality of human interconnectedness.

Pope John Paul II in his 1994 "Letter to Families" proposed a positive meaning of individual identity, based on the nature of the family as a "communion of persons."[12] Children are key to this understanding, as they show the world that human dignity is not measured by how useful a person is to others. The newborn baby merits protective love not for what she does, but for who she *is*—a gift from God. "Could this frail and helpless being, totally dependent upon its parents and completely entrusted to them, be seen in any other way?"[13]

Sadly, abusers *do* see children in another way: not as gifts to be valued for the children's own sake, but as objects for use. John Paul had very strong words for such a mindset: "The person can never be considered a means to an end; above all never a means of 'pleasure.'"[14] Use is "the opposite of love"; it denies that which "is central to the identity of every man and every woman. This identity consists in the *capacity to live in truth and love;* even more, it consists in the need of truth and love as an essential dimension of the life of the person."[15]

One can see in this light how abuse, which creates an atmosphere of lying and mistrust, prevents children from developing their identity in an environment of truth and love.

■ ■ ■

During the six years following her kidnapping, from when she was seven to when she was thirteen, Bakhita was bought and sold several times. One can only imagine how humiliating it must have been for this young girl to be treated as a commodity. Time after time, she was forced to stand naked before prospective masters—strangers who, while carefully avoiding making eye contact with her, would look her up and down, prod her, and talk to her master about her as if she were not there.

In today's America, there is a small but vocal group of adults who claim that a nudist environment is good for children. They argue that it is healthy for kids to be, like Adam and Eve before the Fall, "naked without shame." I was raised in such an environment; so too was Molly Jong-Fast, daughter of bestselling feminist author Erica Jong. Molly recalls in *Girl [Maladjusted]* that, as a young girl, she was "traumatized" by a pornographic image displayed in her home.[16] What advocates of social nudism fail to acknowledge is that even in cultures where nakedness is the norm, people still feel shame when attention is focused on their genitalia. This kind of shame is not the negative kind, born of the mistaken belief that the body is "dirty." Rather, it is, in the words of Karol Wojtyla (before he became Pope John Paul II), "a natural form of self-defense for the person against the danger of descending or being pushed into the position of being an object for sexual use."[17] It is natural for human beings to want to be seen not as mere bodies, but as persons. If that is true for adults, even in primitive cultures, how much more for children—who, as we have seen, find their identity through parents' affirming them in their personhood. Bakhita experienced the depths of depersonalization.

Bakhita's masters in her early years of slavery were all violent, but the worst were the ruthless wife and daughter of a Turkish military general. "In the whole three years I was in their service, I don't recall having got through a single day without a beating: no sooner did my wounds heal than more lashes rained down on my back—without my even knowing why."[18]

In addition to the beatings, it was the wish of the general's daughter that her slaves should have "tattoos"—not the kind made with ink, but patterns cut into their bodies. Details of the tattooing—which, as with all the major traumas of her young life, Bakhita remembered perfectly—are too harrowing to relate here. In short, from the age of about eleven when the cutting took place, Bakhita bore 114 scars from the "tattoos" alone—six on her breasts, sixty on her stomach, and forty-eight on her right arm.

The mutilation that the young saint endured on her breasts certainly places her among victims of the most violent sexual abuse. At the same time, all the cuts Bakhita received serve to deepen her kinship even with those whose abuse was not violent. I have in mind the many survivors who, in later life, tried to relieve their emotional pain through harming themselves.

Psychologists know that self-mutilation, such as cutting, "has been found to occur among recent or former victims of child sexual abuse."[19] Those who harm themselves seek to "reduce the psychic tension associated with extremely negative affect, guilt, intense depersonalization, feelings of helplessness, and/or painfully fragmented thought processes—states all too common among survivors of severe sexual abuse."

Those were my feelings during my late teens and twenties, when I suffered from frequent temptations to cut myself and occasionally gave in. I remember wanting to punish myself, wanting to feel physical pain to take my mind off emotional pain, and, most of all, just wanting to bring all those feelings that were eating at me to a head. Those feelings inside were like a cancer. Somehow I thought if I could bring them out, even at the price of some physical pain, I could rest for a while until they troubled me again.

I mention this in connection with St. Josephine Bakhita because there is a long tradition of calling saints patrons of psychological or medical conditions not because they had those actual conditions, but because they underwent experiences *like* them. St. Maximilian Kolbe, who never abused substances in his life, is considered a patron saint for recovering drug addicts—because the Nazis killed him by lethal injection. St. Denis of Paris is a patron of headache sufferers not because he ever had a migraine, but because he underwent the ultimate headache—decapitation. In the same way, St. Josephine Bakhita's experience of mutilation places her in fellowship with those who have engaged in cutting, even though her own cuts were not self-inflicted. After all, no one really *wants* to cut herself. The desire to self-harm is a compulsion born of extreme mental pain. It is a kind of slavery from within.

Yet, what truly makes Bakhita a patron for all who have endured affliction is not that she was a slave, but that she was *redeemed*. If her early life was a case study in abuse and suffering, her adult life, as we will see, is a case study in healing and forgiveness.

■ ■ ■

The journey of healing, to be effective, must include what spiritual theologians call a "purification of memory." This does not have to include reliving the details of traumatic events; indeed, it shouldn't, if the pain of recalling them is too much to bear. However, it does require the willingness to enter into the past so that we might disentangle traumatic events from events that were *not* traumatic. When we do this, we reclaim the hidden treasures that are rightfully ours. One hidden treasure from my past is Passover.

Following my parents' divorce, there were several years during my childhood when my mother, while continuing to belong to a Jewish temple, explored some New Age movements. Since Mom often brought me along to her activities, my young mind absorbed some messages that could be difficult, if not impossible, to reconcile. On Friday night, at a Jewish temple, we would pray the *Shema*—"Hear O Israel: the Lord our God, the Lord is One" (Dt 6:4 NIV)—but on early Tuesday morning, during a kundalini yoga class at the local ashram, we would chant mantras invoking Guru Nanak.

Although I liked it that my mother wanted to include me in her spiritual explorations—it made me feel special and grown-up—something deep within me longed for stability. Having gone through the upheaval of divorce, I wanted to feel like there was something good and true in the world that would last—a love that would not go away.

That was why it meant so much to me that, every year throughout my childhood, our family—my mother, my sister, and I—either hosted or attended a Passover Seder, the ceremonial meal commemorating God's deliverance of the Israelites from slavery in Egypt. I loved the sights, sounds, and tastes of our Passover tradition. There was the special gilt-edged Seder plate, a beautiful wedding gift that Mom was able to keep after the divorce. There were the foods that we only got to eat at Passover time, like chocolate-covered matzo (much more delicious than it sounds), macaroons, and *haroset*, a chunky paste made with apples, cinnamon, walnuts, and sweet red Mogen David wine. There was Elijah's cup, the silver goblet filled with wine that stood at an empty place setting, waiting for the part of the meal when it was said that the spirit of the Old Testament prophet entered the room. We kids were told that if we looked hard enough at the cup when Elijah was invited in, we would see the wine level go down as though Elijah had taken a sip.

But what I remember most of all was how all our family members and friends around the table took part in the reading of the *Haggadah*, the ancient Seder service combining the story of the Exodus with joyful prayers thanking God for the gift of freedom.

There was something special about knowing that Jews around the world that night were telling the same story and praying the same prayers. For one evening, the feelings of isolation that dogged me throughout my childhood were dispelled by a sense of kinship and community. Likewise, having had my family split in two, I was comforted to take part in a tradition that went back thousands of years, to the days when God spoke to Moses "face to face, as a man speaks to his friend" (Ex 33:11). Everyday life was full of changes and upheavals; here there was continuity, the sense of being part of something extending to all places and all times.

If someone had asked me to draw a picture of this feeling, I would have sketched a long, narrow Seder table with me and my family seated at its center. Seated at the left end of the table would have been Jews from countries to our geographic left, including Japan. (I knew from the *Book of Lists* that there were indeed Jews in Japan—one thousand of them, which sounded like a lot.) Likewise, I would have populated the other end with Jews from our geographic right—giving the French one a beret and a baguette-shaped piece of matzo.

Then I would have had to represent the sense of history. So, above the table, at the very top of the drawing, I would have drawn a lightning bolt zapping the Ten Commandments into tablets of stone. Below it would have been Moses, his arms outstretched to receive the Law. Below him, in totem-pole fashion, would have been people representing generations of Jews, descending chronologically, from biblical prophets to medieval rabbis, to nineteenth-century Russian peasant women in babushkas. Intersecting with the image of me at the long Passover table, the line would have continued downward to future generations—the last of them dressed in futuristic spacesuits like in a *Jetsons* cartoon.

Had I drawn that image during one of my childhood Seders, I would have offered it to my mother, who would have loved it; she always encouraged creativity. I imagine her proudly passing the drawing down the Seder table, eliciting "oohs" and "aahs" at my artistic genius—that is, until my know-it-all sister, five years my senior, pipes up, "Why did you draw Passover in the shape of a cross?"

■ ■ ■

Relief came for St. Josephine Bakhita in 1882 at the age of thirteen when the Turkish general sold her to Callisto Legnani, the Italian consul in the Sudanese capital of

Khartoum, who wanted a slave to assist his housekeeper. The saint would later recall with wonder how, in her new household, "there were no scoldings, no punishments, no beatings! I couldn't believe I was enjoying so much peace and quiet."[20]

Three years later, when civil unrest erupted in Sudan, Legnani and a fellow businessman, Augusto Michieli, returned with his household to Italy, taking lodgings in a guest house in Genoa. There, Bakhita changed hands once again, as Legnani gave the now eighteen-year-old slave to Michieli's wife, Maria Turina, as a present. The Michielis took her into their family home in Zianigo, a small village outside Venice. When Maria Turina had a daughter, Mimmina, the following year, Bakhita became the girl's nanny. "The baby came to love me dearly, and I naturally came to feel a similar affection for her."[21]

It was not long, however, before business called Augusto back to Sudan. He owned a hotel in the port city of Suakin that soon came to require his full attention. After two years of mostly living apart, the Michielis decided to sell their Italian property so that they could live together in Suakin full-time.

The sale turned out to be a long, drawn-out process, taking a full year. When it was almost completed, Maria Turina decided to travel to Suakin on her own to spend some private time with her husband. On the advice of her husband's business administrator, Illuminato Cecchini— who, unlike the nonreligious Michielis, was a devout Catholic—she left Bakhita and Mimmina at a home in Venice run by the Canossian Sisters. The home was a catechumenate, a place where adult non-Catholics, who were usually foreigners without local family, could live while they received instruction to enter the Church. But Bakhita would say that her encounter with Christ actually began a few weeks prior to the move, when Cecchini, during one of his frequent visits to the Michieli home, presented her with a small silver crucifix:

> Giving me the crucifix he kissed it with devotion, then explained to me that Jesus Christ, Son of God, died for us. I didn't know what it was, but, impelled by a mysterious force, I hid it in case my mistress took it off me. Before then I had never hidden anything, because I was never attached to anything. I remember how I used to look at it in secret, and feel inside myself something I couldn't explain.[22]

Upon arriving with Mimmina at the catechumenate, Bakhita agreed to let the Canossians teach her about the faith. The women were officially known as sisters, but the customary form of address for them was "mother." As they taught the African young woman, by then nearly twenty years old, about the love of the Father, Bakhita began to find her identity within the family of God. "Those holy mothers instructed me with heroic patience, and brought me into a relationship with that God whom, ever since I was a child, I had felt in my heart without knowing who he was."[23]

Pope Benedict, in his encyclical *Spe Salvi* ("Saved by Hope"), has some beautiful insights into what this new relationship meant for the saint:

> Here, after the terrifying "masters" who had owned her up to that point, Bakhita came to know a totally different kind of "master"—in Venetian dialect, which she was now learning,

she used the name *"paron"* for the living God,
the God of Jesus Christ. Up to that time she
had known only masters who despised and
maltreated her, or at best considered her a useful slave. Now, however, she heard that there
is a *"paron"* above all masters, the Lord of all
lords, and that this Lord is good, goodness in
person. She came to know that this Lord even
knew her, that he had created her—that he actually loved her. She too was loved, and by none
other than the supreme *"Paron,"* before whom
all other masters are themselves no more than
lowly servants. She was known and loved and
she was awaited.[24]

Yet, as she prepared for baptism, Bakhita's joy was
tempered by painful memories. A young girl named
Giulia, who used to visit the catechumenate to play with
Mimmina, noticed that "Bakhita was always smiling—and
yet there was something odd about the smile: it was a kind
smile, but it wasn't a happy one."[25]

Bakhita found comfort in praying, often contemplating
a crucifix as she spoke inwardly to the One who understood her even when others did not. As Pope Benedict
writes, here was a "master [who] had himself accepted
the destiny of being flogged and now he was waiting for
her 'at the Father's right hand.'"[26] Knowing this made suffering bearable, because "now she had 'hope'—no longer
simply the modest hope of finding masters who would be
less cruel, but the great hope: 'I am definitively loved and
whatever happens to me—I am awaited by this Love. And
so my life is good.' Through the knowledge of this hope
she was 'redeemed,' no longer a slave, but a free child of
God."[27] That is why, when Maria Turina returned from

Suakin to claim Mimmina and her slave, Bakhita stunned her mistress by insisting on staying put. "She did not wish to be separated again from her '*Paron.*'"[28]

Maria Turina protested furiously, but the law was on Bakhita's side: Italy did not permit slavery. Although heartbroken at being separated from Mimmina, Bakhita was, in her own words, "satisfied I hadn't given in."[29]

On January 9, 1890, Bakhita was baptized with the Christian name Josephine; she then was confirmed and received First Communion. Giulia, the girl who had played with Mimmina, was "overwhelmed to see Bakhita's radiant joy: the sadness was gone, and she seemed completely transfigured."[30] From then on, according to her official Vatican biography, the saint "was often seen kissing the baptismal font and saying: 'Here, I became a daughter of God!'"[31]

Bakhita would become a Canossian Sister, much beloved by the children at the institute's schools. They loved to hear her tell her life story, knowing that it would end with her seated contently before them as their Mother "Moretta"—"Black Mother." Sometimes the younger children would tug at the flowing right sleeve of her habit, begging for a peek at her patchwork of scars. But if they expressed any anger at the slaveowners who had treated her so cruelly, she was quick to correct them: "If I were to meet those who kidnapped me, or even those who tortured me, I would kneel down and kiss their hands. Because, if those things had not happened, I would not have become a Christian and would not be a sister today."[32]

■ ■ ■

Does God want this particular brand of sanctity from us, where we would actually kneel down and kiss the hands of our worst abusers? No, not literally—evildoers should never be rewarded for their actions—and I don't believe Bakhita meant her words that way. What's more, every person's story is different. Some of us can indeed reach out to those who hurt us the most, allowing ourselves to be emotionally vulnerable for the greater good of reconciliation and healing. For others of us, the most loving thing we can do for our abusers is to keep them from having any opportunity to abuse us ever again.

While in these matters we should, whenever possible, seek advice from someone we trust, no one else can decide our course of action for us. The choice of whether it is best for us to initiate contact with our abuser, or seek to maintain distance, is ultimately between us and God. Perhaps that is what Bakhita meant when, speaking to a fellow sister about her life as a slave, she said somewhat mysteriously, "There are things which only the Lord has seen. One can neither speak of them nor write of them."[33]

Yet, in another way, I believe God does call every one of us to be thankful for our past. We may not be capable of kissing our abusers' hands. But we will one day want to kiss the hands of Jesus—who, while not willing the abuse (for God never positively wills evil), permitted it to happen, knowing he would bring good out of it. Proof that good *can* come out of it is witnessed in the lives of saints like Bakhita. The same proof is manifest in the life of any victim who now feels God's goodness in his heart. No matter how much we may be hurting, that goodness is surely present if we long to draw nearer to divine love. We would not have that longing at all if God were not in our hearts already, drawing us nearer to him. This is the message that Blessed John Paul II wanted people to take from St. Josephine Bakhita's life, as he said in his homily for her beatification:

> Man sometimes thinks: "The Lord has aban-
> doned us! He has forgotten us" (Is 49:14).
> And God answers with the words of the great
> Prophet: *"Can a woman forget her own baby,* and
> not love the child she bore? Even if a mother
> should forget her child, I will never forget you.
> *I have written your name on the palms of my hands"*
> (Is 49:15–16). Yes, on the palms of the hands of
> Christ, pierced by the nails of the Crucifixion. *The
> name of each one of you is written on those palms.*[34]

■ ■ ■

As a child, I was intrigued by the Seder's notion of a kind of timeless time. In describing the Exodus, the Haggadah isn't just retelling a past event. It insists, again and again, that the Exodus is *now*. It isn't just about the deliverance of Jews thousands of years ago; it is about our own deliverance today. "*We* were slaves," it says. "In every generation, each person must see himself as if he personally went out of Egypt." This Seder, it says, "is because of what the Almighty did for me when I left Egypt."

Year after year, the Haggadah's multiple layers of meaning never ceased to fascinate me. Literally speaking, the Exodus was a historical event, tied forever to a particular time and place. Figuratively speaking, it is present now and ever will be, in all times and all places, wherever the People of God are present "to thank, to laud, to praise, to glorify" the One who redeemed us.

That same timeless time that I contemplated with endless fascination as a child—that is what I now contemplate in the Mass. I am not literally at the Incarnation, at Calvary, or at the empty tomb. Yet, as I kneel before the Real Presence of Christ in the Eucharist, all those events are now before me. Those and all the events of Christ's life are part of his memory, in the Ignatian sense: they make up who he is. What's more, through him—through Christ in me, as I receive the consecrated Host—they become part of *my* memory. At the same time, all the events of my life—my memory, my identity—are present to Christ, as they have always been. If I ask him, with the words of Ignatius, "Take, O Lord, and receive all my liberty, my memory, my understanding, and my whole will," his memory can purify mine.[35]

■ ■ ■

If you look up the word *suscipe* in a Latin dictionary, you will find that its main meaning is "take" or "raise," but it also means to take up a newborn child as one's own. This refers to an early Roman custom in which the father had the right to repudiate a baby. Immediately after birth, the child was placed at its father's feet. If instead of being lifted up by the father, the newborn was left on the ground, he or she was excluded from the family.

And so it is that, when praying the *Suscipe*, I discover my identity in Christ as Bakhita did. I am the beloved child of God, longing to be taken into the arms of my Heavenly Father. The image adds new meaning to St. Paul's emphatic teaching, "For those who are led by the Spirit of God are children of God. For you did not receive a spirit of slavery to fall back into fear, but you received a spirit of adoption through which we cry, '*Abba*, Father!'" (Rom 8:15 NAB).

CHAPTER 2

The Love That Shelters

Opening our hearts to the Sacred Heart—with Mary, Mother of Hope

> He was thankful that he had known so much
> want, and gone through so much suffering, for
> it made him appreciate his present happiness
> and the loveliness of everything about him all
> the more. . . . He shook his feathers, stretched
> his slender neck, and in the joy of his heart said,
> "I never dreamed of so much happiness when
> I was the ugly, despised duckling!"
>
> —Hans Christian Andersen
> "The Ugly Duckling"

When I was ten years old, one unexpectedly graced evening began when my mother—then working as a school psychologist—invited me to go with her to a school where she had to meet with some parents. I was happy to come along, especially when she assured me we would stop at my favorite taco joint on the way home.

Arriving at the school, Mom took me to a playroom where a delicate little blonde girl about two years younger than me sat on the orange rug. Her eyes were downcast and she was dully fingering some building blocks. Mom explained to me quietly that this girl's mother was one of the parents at the meeting, and wouldn't I be nice to her? Then she disappeared into a room down the hall, promising to return in an hour or so, and I was left alone with this strange, sullen girl.

Following Mom's instructions, I tried to engage my new playmate in conversation, only to be met by stony silence. She would not even make eye contact. (On the way home, I would learn from my mother that she was "autistic" and "emotionally disturbed.") But there wasn't anything else to do, so I kept reaching out to her, offering her dolls and other toys from the playroom's stores, and inviting her to play along with me.

The girl accepted the toys I offered, but went off into her own world with them. I played alongside her and pretended we were playing together even though we weren't, keeping up my end of the friendly chatter just because she was there and I was bored. And I wondered what was taking my mother so long.

An hour passed and still my mother had not returned. It was then that I got the idea to play "telephone." I'm not sure why. Maybe I was trying to trick the girl into talking. Or maybe I just felt like doing something creative and figured that, even if she remained silent, she might at least enjoy pretending someone was phoning her.

At any rate, I remember handing the girl a toy phone. I don't recall whether I also had one or if I just mimed, using my clenched hand as a receiver. I do remember holding a toy receiver or my hand to my ear and saying, *"Brrring! Brrring!"*

Nothing could have prepared me for what happened next.

The little girl straightaway picked up her phone's receiver, as natural as can be: "Hello?"

I was stunned, but managed to say a few words in reply. And she just started chattering away, in the sweetest little-girl voice. Her speech sounded perfectly normal. Anyone hearing her at that moment would have thought she was an ordinary kid.

Once she got started talking, the girl pretty much went back into her own world. We didn't really have a conversation so much as she talked at me. Even so, she seemed to really enjoy the "game."

My mother, returning from her meeting, was surprised to find me euphoric. As soon as we started to make our way to her car, I told her how I had gotten my playmate to talk. Knowing the extent of the girl's problems, Mom was shocked and delighted to learn I had managed in some way to get through to her. We spent the ride home talking—in between taco bites—about how I would grow up to become a great psychologist.

Looking back, I see that my reaction contained a lot more pride than it did love. I felt like a clever fairytale heroine who had solved the riddle of the Sphinx. At the same time, deep down, my heart rejoiced at the mysterious bonding that had taken place. When I entered that playroom, the girl and I were two isolated individuals. By the time I left, we had *connected*.

My joy, however, was not complete. The girl had responded to me at a distance, but not to my face. Our connection did not reach the level of communion.

I think about that episode now because it reminds me of what it is like to learn how to communicate with God after suffering childhood sexual abuse.

At first, we don't talk about the abuse with anyone. Alone with the memory of our experience, we are as isolated, vulnerable, and unhappy as that quiet girl with the sad eyes. Or we may try to tell someone, only to find that person unworthy of our trust. Looking for understanding, we meet instead with blame and shame, becoming even more isolated than before.

As time goes on, we may finally be able to open up to a trusted friend, family member, or therapist—someone who tries, as best he or she can, to respond in an appropriately loving way. This person becomes for us a "telephone," a human instrument through which we become connected in a new and special way to divine love, "because love is from God" (1 Jn 4:7).

The saints can be intermediaries for us in this way as well. In fact, the Communion of Saints that we profess in the Apostles' Creed—which includes all the Church's members, whether on earth, in purgatory, or in heaven—is much more than a mere "telephone." As the Mystical Body of Christ, it is more like a telecommunications network transmitting grace 24/7. The *Catechism of the Catholic Church*, quoting St. Thomas Aquinas, describes it as "one body," "governed by one and the same Spirit," in which "the riches of Christ are communicated to all the members, through the sacraments" and "the good of each is communicated to the others" (*CCC* 947).

But if we are to be truly healed, we need to do more than approach God through other people. We need to come to him directly, with open heart, in prayer. For many of us, that may seem like the hardest thing to do. As was the case for that vulnerable little girl in the playroom, the thought of communicating face-to-face may fill us with fear. We may fear he will judge us, or that he will demand too much of us, or—and this is, I think, the worst fear of all—that he will meet us with cold indifference.

Because the Church does not want anyone to let such fears prevent him or her from approaching the divine "source of all consolation," it points us to the Sacred Heart of Jesus—"our peace and our reconciliation," as the Litany of the Sacred Heart prays.

■ ■ ■

Growing up Jewish, I found devotion to the Sacred Heart to be one of the odder aspects of the Catholic faith. Even if Jesus was God, why should one of his organs be set apart for veneration?

It wasn't until I studied the *Catechism* that it began to make sense. In everyday conversation, the heart is more than just any body part. It represents the center of our being, the source of our will, the axis of our love. The *Catechism* notes that, while God's love is infinite, "Christ's body was finite" (CCC 476). The Sacred Heart, then, provides us with a human gateway to the mystery of divine love, enabling us to begin to conceive what is ultimately beyond our imagination.

> [In] the body of Jesus "we see our God made visible and so are caught up in love of the God we cannot see." The individual characteristics of Christ's body express the divine person of God's Son. . . . He has loved us all with a human heart. For this reason, the Sacred Heart of Jesus, pierced by our sins and for our salvation, "is quite rightly considered the chief sign and symbol of that . . . love with which the divine Redeemer continually loves the eternal Father and all human beings" without exception.[1]

Although these words of the *Catechism* showed me that veneration of the Sacred Heart was reasonable, what really won me over to the devotion was a *visual* catechism. I discovered it one day in 2009, while exploring the campus of Georgetown University, a healthy walk from my home in Washington, DC. It was in the form of a trio of stunning stained-glass windows on the north wall of the Dahlgren Chapel of the Sacred Heart.

Consecrated in 1893, the chapel was erected by John and Elizabeth Dahlgren in memory of their infant son Joseph, who had died of pneumonia. Elizabeth, a cousin of the Philadelphia nun who would become known as St. Katharine Drexel, traveled to Munich, Germany, so that she might personally direct the construction of the chapel's stained-glass windows. Seeing how beautifully the windows depict the consoling love of the Sacred Heart, I imagine that the bereaved young mother wanted, like St. Paul, to comfort others with the comfort she herself had received from God (2 Cor 1:4).

The left-hand window of the Sacred Heart–themed triptych shows Jesus instituting the Eucharist at the Last Supper. From my perspective, he is looking directly at me. His left hand is holding the bread against his heart, and his right hand is raised in blessing. St. John is seated close at his side, leaning on the inside of Jesus' left shoulder, so close as to hear the beating of the Sacred Heart. His eyes are fixed on the Eucharist.

No other disciples are visible in the narrow window, but I see the back of an empty chair on the side of the table that faces Jesus—apparently the one Judas left when he hurried out to betray the Lord. Jesus seems to be inviting me to put myself in that empty chair, so that I may receive the Eucharist from his own hands and give his Sacred Heart my love to make up for the hatred of the betrayer.

Seeing St. John at Jesus' side, I imagine I am witnessing the moment in John's gospel when the Lord urged us to make the love of his Heart our own: "I give you a new commandment: love one another. As I have loved you, so you also should love one another" (Jn 13:34 NAB). And in that love he offers the greatest gift of all: "Peace I leave with you; my peace I give to you. Not as the world gives do I give it to you. Do not let your hearts be troubled or afraid" (Jn 14:27 NAB).

The verse takes me back to the time when, as a child, I first took a curious look at the gospels. I remember how the phrase jumped out at me: "Not as the world gives." *Someone understands*, I thought. Someone understands that there is something very wrong with the way the world gives peace. The world gives peace only to take it away unexpectedly at any moment. What I longed for was true peace, a *living* peace—a peace I could enjoy forever.

■ ■ ■

After contemplating the first window in the Dahlgren Chapel's triptych, my eyes move to the center one: Jesus on the Cross. The centurion does not appear in the scene, but he has left his mark: a spear wound in Jesus' side. A few red trickles remain at the spot where blood and water flowed a moment ago from the Savior's pierced heart. Mary stands at the left side of the Cross, her face downcast, with an expression of mourning so deep as to be beyond emotion. Judging by the dark circles around her eyes, it seems as though she has suffered with Jesus through his entire Passion—even, somehow, in his agony the night before.

John is at the right side of the Cross, leaning forward to Mary, arms open as though to enfold her in a protective embrace. He is following the last commandment of Jesus' earthly life. The words spoken by the Savior just a few moments ago seem to hang in the air: "Behold, your mother (Jn 19:27 RSV)." It is as though Jesus is ensuring that his peace—the peace of the Sacred Heart—once given, does not leave us for one moment. Even as he departs for three days, to return in the Resurrection, he remains with the human community through his Mystical Body, the Church, whose Mother and pre-eminent member is Mary (*Lumen Gentium* 53).

Finally, I turn my gaze to the last window of the triptych, and there I find an image that must come as a surprise to some visitors, as it depicts a scene not in the Bible. It takes place inside a room with windows revealing the beginnings of a sunrise. Here, as with the Crucifixion, Our Lady is on the left and the apostle John is on the right, with Jesus in the midst of them. Mary looks to be several years older than she was at the Crucifixion, but still beautiful. This time, she is not standing, but kneeling in a position reminiscent of the way artists depict her *fiat*—her "yes"—to the angel Gabriel. Her face is tilted upward and her hands are clasped with fingertips pointing toward heaven. John stands on a step above Mary, facing her. As in the other two windows, Jesus is at the center—but this time, he is in the form of the Eucharist, held in John's right hand. In other words, the third window shows the apostle John giving Holy Communion to the Mother of God.

With that quietly dramatic image, the Dahlgren Chapel windows' visual catechism of the Sacred Heart comes to a profound conclusion. Let's take a moment to review:

- Window 1: Jesus gives us his Sacred Heart through the Eucharist, at the Last Supper, as a permanent memorial of his approaching Passion.

- Window 2: The Sacred Heart triumphs on the Cross, as Jesus gives his physical body "for the life of the world" (Jn 6:15)—and in our own hearts, as Jesus calls Mary to become Mother of his Mystical Body, the Church. "[The] motherhood of her who bore Christ finds a 'new' continuation in the Church and through

the Church, symbolized and represented by John"
(John Paul II, "Mother of the Redeemer").

* Window 3: Through Holy Communion, the Sacred
  Heart in the Eucharist—the same one poured out
  for us on the Cross—and the Sacred Heart in the
  Church are joined in an exchange of love. "If any
  one love me . . . my Father will love him, and we
  will come to him, and will make our abode with
  him" (Jn 14:23 DV).

■ ■ ■

I remain haunted by the beauty of that last window. It
conveys Mary's experience in a way that is, for me, deeply
cathartic. Here is a woman who, during her Son's Passion,
endured the most intense emotional trauma any human
being could undergo and survive. The fact that, at a time
when all but one of the disciples had fled, she was able to
remain standing by the Cross, pouring out her heart for
her Son as he poured out his own Heart for the world, is
in itself something of a miracle.

The window shows us Mary at a time when her memory contained not only the pain of the Crucifixion, but also
the joy of the Resurrection. But it also shows us something
more: Mary in the present moment, living in the tension
between earth and heaven. That pilgrim experience is part
of every Christian's life; we know Jesus is present with
us, but must rely on faith as "the evidence of things not
seen" (Heb 11:1 NAB). Yet, how much greater must that
tension have been for Mary, the first human being ever to
see Jesus' face, when it came to pass that she could see him
only under the veil of the Eucharist.

I see all those memories, the pain and the joy, as well as the tension of the present moment, in the expression of longing on Mary's face as she receives her Son in Holy Communion. It is the same spirit of expectation that Pope Benedict described when he wrote of Mary after Pentecost that "[she remained] in the midst of the disciples as their Mother, as the Mother of hope."[2] Instead of letting herself be defined by the three hours when the sun went black, she is defined by the Easter morning when the light of the resurrected Christ, who is the "Light from Light," dawned upon the world, never to depart. She knows, as our Lord told the disciples on the way to Emmaus, that it was indeed "necessary that the Messiah should suffer these things and enter into his glory" (Lk 24:26 NAB).

The resurrection, then, does not wipe out Mary's memory of the Passion. Rather, it *completes* her experience, enabling her to properly integrate the trauma into her identity. Her past pain becomes an integral part of her present joy.

Mary's experience parallels the growth process that medical experts say is essential if victims of traumatic stress are to find healing:

> The key element of the psychotherapy of people with PTSD is the integration of the alien, the unacceptable, the terrifying, and the incomprehensible into their self-concepts. . . . Traumatic memories need to become like memories of everyday experience; that is, they need to be modified and transformed by being placed in their proper context and restructured into a meaningful narrative.[3]

While agreeing with the experts' advice, I have to smile
at that last sentence in light of Mary's experience. It is quite
the understatement to say she managed to restructure her
memories into a "meaningful narrative." More accurately,
she continually allowed God to guide her in such restruc-
turing—offering him her memory, her intellect, and her
whole will (to borrow a phrase from St. Ignatius's *Suscipe*).
In this way, although one needs not speak of "purification"
regarding the woman who was immaculate from conception, Mary's response to pain is a model for those of us
who seek purification of memory.

Long before the Passion, the Gospel of Luke shows
us the beginning of Mary's allowing God to reshape how
she perceives her past experiences. We find it in the episode when a distraught Mary and Joseph, after three days'
searching, find the twelve-year-old Jesus in the temple.
Jesus says to them, "Why were you looking for me? Did
you not know that I must be in my Father's house?" (Lk
2:49 NAB). Fr. Angelo Mary Geiger, F.I., a priest of the
Franciscans of the Immaculate, points out that Jesus'
words give Mary an interpretational key: "Three days,
the Father's house." After that, "she won't be surprised
again. The next time Jesus is gone for three days, she
will know exactly where to find him."[4] That is because,
as Luke wrote, even though Mary and Joseph "did not
understand" the Lord's words at that moment, Mary "kept
all these things in her heart" (Lk 2:50, 51).

Fr. José Granados observes that "[in] a sense, this marks
the difference between Mary and the other characters of
Luke's Gospel. Like the disciples, Mary did not immediately grasp the meaning of Jesus' words; the difference

is that she retained his answers and kept meditating on them, while the others were afraid to ask."[5]

There indeed lies a clue as to why Mary had the strength and courage to remain standing at Jesus' side throughout the Crucifixion, while all the disciples except John could not bear to be present. She had already begun to restructure her understanding in light of what had been revealed to her of God's plan. Keeping Jesus' words in her heart enabled her to move forward even when she could not yet see how the present trauma would be resolved.

Mary's fortitude came not from forgetting her past suffering, but from remembering it in a *new way*. She exemplifies the truth expressed in an essay by Cardinal Joseph Ratzinger before he became Pope Benedict XVI—"memory awakens hope":

> In one of his Christmas stories Charles Dickens tells of a man who lost his emotional memory; that is, he lost the whole chain of feelings and thoughts he had acquired in the encounter with human suffering. This extinction of the memory of love is presented to him as liberation from the burden of the past, but it becomes clear immediately that the whole person has been changed: now, when he meets with suffering, no memories of kindness are stirred within him. Since his memory has dried up, the source of kindness within him has also disappeared. He has become cold and spreads coldness around him. In other words, it is only the person who has memories who can hope. . . .
>
> Recently a counselor who spends much of his time talking with people on the verge of despair was speaking in similar terms about his

own work: if his client succeeds in recalling a
memory of some good experience, he may once
again be able to believe in goodness and thus
relearn hope; then there is a way out of despair.[6]

The process Ratzinger describes by which we "relearn
hope" mirrors St. Josephine Bakhita's experience of purification of memory. As we saw in chapter 1, the trauma of
her kidnapping caused her to forget her own name, yet she
held onto her childhood recollection of gazing with awe at
"the sun, the moon and the stars," wondering "[who] could
be the Master of these beautiful things," and desiring "to see
him, to know him and to pay him homage."[7]

I remember one moment as a child when I felt a similar
sense of joy. It must have occurred when my parents were
still together, because, in picturing that afternoon, I realize
I could not have been more than five years old.

My family then lived in a house in Galveston, Texas,
right on the bay. It was a cloudy day, and I was sitting in our
back yard, looking out over the gray ripples of the water.
My imagination turned, as it often did at the time, to my
favorite pastime—reading Charles Schulz's *Peanuts* comic
strip. I loved its Charlie Brown character, identifying with
his loneliness.

One of the running themes of *Peanuts* was the question, "Why are we here on earth?" Charlie Brown's stock
answer was, "To make others happy." Lucy responded
to this—quite sensibly, I thought—"What are the others
here for?"

There had to be something more to life, I thought as
I looked out onto the water, than merely making others
happy. Why *are* we here? What is the meaning of life?

Suddenly it hit me with a blinding clarity: *The answer to everything is that we all have to* love *one another. Love means more than making people happy. If everyone truly loved one another, there would be no war, no fighting . . .*

No fighting. As I recall that epiphany, I'm sure it must have occurred during the period when the tension between my parents, which would shortly lead to their separation, was boiling over into heated arguments. Yet, for that one moment, I was like the character in G. K. Chesterton's *The Man Who Was Thursday* who "felt he was in possession of some impossible good news, which made every other thing a triviality, but an *adorable* triviality."

I had the urge to dash into the house and share the answer to everything with my mom and dad. But then, even as the urge came to me, a sort of premature cynicism arose. *It's too simple,* I thought. *Surely people have tried it and it didn't work. How silly of me to think adults will take it seriously.* Then I thought about getting a piece of paper and writing the answer down, but likewise nixed that idea. At that time, the only extended piece of writing I had attempted was a fan letter to Charles Schulz, and I proved miserably inept at figuring out where the commas should go. (My solution was to put a comma between every word, just to be on the safe side.)

But the real reason I was reluctant to move from my spot overlooking the water was because I feared that, in the course of walking twenty feet to the sliding doors that opened into our living room, I would forget what I had experienced. It wasn't just a verbal answer that had come to me, but a sense of the numinous. Even as it arrived, it began to slip away.

Years later, I was stunned to discover that C. S. Lewis had experienced an identical sensation when he was a child, which he described in his autobiography *Surprised by Joy*:

> It was a sensation, of course, of desire; but desire for what? . . . Before I knew what I desired, the desire itself was gone, the whole glimpse withdrawn, the world turned commonplace again, or only stirred by a longing for the longing that had just ceased. It had taken only a moment of time; and in a certain sense everything else that had ever happened to me was insignificant in comparison.[8]

Faced with the realization that I could neither hold onto the answer I had received, nor convey it in a way that would be meaningful for others, I resolved to remember at least that the experience had taken place. For one moment, I had experienced the joy of certain knowledge. No one could take that experience away from me.

During the ensuing years, I went through many things—some at the hands of others, and some, when I was a rather lost young adult, of my own making—that caused me to despair of ever finding such joy again. But the longing to re-experience it remained.

When I eventually received the gift of faith in Christ, I was able to recognize in that Galveston afternoon the same thing C. S. Lewis ultimately recognized in his own childhood experiences of joy. It was a promise of good things, however distant—a foretaste of future happiness, even a hint of heaven. Possessing it in my memory gave me a needed toehold into a part of my past that had, over the course of the intervening years, become overlaid with trauma and loss. As with the other positive childhood memories that I would rediscover over time, such as the Passover Seder, it added a comforting sense of continuity to my new life in Christ. After years of seeking a foundation for my sense of self, I finally discovered my identity, and realized with surprise that the rags of my childhood sufferings had turned into an evening gown of mature character. Like the "ugly duckling" in the Hans Christian Andersen tale, I had become who I truly was.

■ ■ ■

For those of us who have trouble following Ratzinger's advice of "recalling a memory of some good experience," there is always one good experience whose memory is before us at all times. It is the experience of continually being sustained in existence by God: what I called in chapter 1 "the love we forget."

Each of us came to be because our heavenly Father loved us and willed us into existence. Admittedly, if we have not been blessed with parents or guardians who embodied God's love for us, we may have trouble internalizing this truth. I know this from my own experience, having tried throughout my childhood, teen years, and young adulthood to believe people when they told me, "God loves you." Many times, especially after my mother gave up her New Age beliefs for Christian faith, I would go to church, thinking that perhaps I would receive faith and hope by osmosis. It didn't work, because I was confusing Christian faith with a feeling—which it is not. It is a *lived reality*.

At every Sunday Mass, Catholics recite the Creed: "I believe in one God . . ." In the original Greek, the word *eis*, translated as "in," literally bears a meaning closer to "into." What we are really saying is not merely that we make the intellectual choice to believe, but that we believe with *understanding*—an understanding that actually draws us into union with God, the object of our faith. Faith, on this account, is more than mere acknowledgment of the Creator. It is a dynamic principle that draws us forward to God, carried by grace, whether we feel its operations or not.

There have been moments in my life when I have been blessed with the consoling feeling of the Lord's presence. It is an unspeakably beautiful sensation, and I long to have it again. But I have come to realize that, in the long run, there is something even more consoling than momentarily sensing the nearness of God. It is the sure knowledge that regardless of how I may feel at any given moment (for feelings, as we all know, can come and go), my heart is united to God because I *believe*.

For many saints and blesseds, including John of the Cross, Thérèse of Lisieux, and Mother Teresa, the road to sanctity entailed a long "dark night of the soul" when they found themselves unable to feel any joy in prayer— or, in some cases, unable even to pray at all. Yet, because those holy men and women continued to believe, "hoping against hope" (Rom 4:18 NAB), their times of dryness did not detract from their spiritual walk. On the contrary, they continued to offer their open hearts to God even when he seemed to be refusing to fill them. In doing so, they became ever more closely conformed to the crucified Christ, who, although he never lost his union with the Father, yet—through his identification with sinful humanity—experienced the agony of separation: "My God, my God, why hast thou forsaken me?" (Mt 27:46).[9]

These saints have taught me that it is not essential that I *feel* loved by God. What matters most is that I accept the undeniable facts of my birth and continued existence as evidence that he cares about me, sustains me, and therefore must have a purpose for me. That evidence, once accepted, cannot help but lead to the deeper truth that—in the words of Pope Benedict—God loves every one of us "with a personal love" (*Deus Caritas Est*). Or, to put it another way, in a saying ascribed to Ethel Waters—the great African American jazz singer who was conceived in rape—"God don't make no junk."

■ ■ ■

A few years ago, near the front door of the Dahlgren Chapel, a newly installed stained-glass window brought a fresh variation to the church's Sacred Heart theme. It depicts one of the Church's newest saints, the nineteenth-century Anglican convert Blessed John Henry Newman, and features his motto, *"Cor ad cor loquitur"*—"Heart speaks to heart."

In one sense, "Heart speaks to heart" represents Newman's belief that "the best preparation for loving the world at large, and loving it duly and wisely, is to cultivate an intimate friendship and affection towards those who are immediately about us."[10] Newman seems to have held permanently before his eyes a kind of joyful vision very like the one I experienced so fleetingly as a child. I had imagined that, if those who were closest to me loved one another, the whole world would love another, and all would be well. Newman proclaimed that "[the] test of our being joined to Christ is love; the test of love towards Christ and his Church, is loving those whom we actually see."[11]

The notion of "being joined to Christ" through love of neighbor brings forth the larger meaning of Newman's motto. It is the message of St. John: "We love because he first loved us" (1 Jn 4:19 NAB). Newman explains that it is through allowing the love of the Sacred Heart to speak to our heart, and letting our heart speak in return, that we become capable of true emotional intimacy with one another: "We know that even our nearest friends enter into us but partially, and [converse] with us only at times; whereas the consciousness of a perfect and enduring Presence, and it alone, keeps the heart open."[12]

CHAPTER 3

The Love That Suffers

Sharing in Christ's Passion— with St. Gemma Galgani and St. Sebastian

> With the sharpness of memory that the souls will have on the Day of Judgment, Helga remembered her life. Every kindness performed toward her, every loving word spoken to her, became terribly real. She understood that it was love that had fought and been victorious in the struggle within her. . . . She realized that she had followed a will greater than her own and that she herself had not been the maker of her own fate. She had been guided and led. She bent her head humbly in front of him who can see into the most secret compartment of our hearts. And in that moment she felt a flame that purified her, the flame of the Holy Ghost.
>
> —Hans Christian Andersen
> "The Bog King's Daughter"

When Christ was hanging upon the Cross, the chief priests, scribes, and elders said, "He saved others; he cannot save himself. He is the King of Israel; let him come down now from the cross, and we will believe in him" (Mt 27:42).

Nearly two thousand years later, my Jewish parents expressed similar sentiments—though minus the

derision—when, at the age of five, I asked them for the
first time about Jesus. I was told that, if he were God, he
would not have been crucified; therefore he was not God.
Mom and Dad did admit Jesus was "a good man," but that
only served to confuse me, since I knew that good men did
not lie, and Jesus said he was the Son of God.

Over time, I discovered that the belief that the Crucifixion was evidence against Jesus' divinity was not unique to
Jews. Popular culture gave abundant evidence that there
were even Christians who were scandalized by the Cross.
Two of the bestselling recordings during my childhood
were the original-cast albums of the musicals *Godspell* and
Jesus Christ Superstar. Neither show depicts the Crucifixion
the way it is described in the Second Eucharistic Prayer
of the Mass, which says Jesus "entered willingly into his
Passion." Instead, they present it as an unwilled end to the
life of a teacher who was only human and not divine. No
one who does not already know the Gospel would gather
from these musicals that Christ's suffering is our salvation;
"by his stripes we were healed" (Is 53:5 NAB).

It was only over time, through the writings of the
saints—that is to say, saintly people like G. K. Chesterton, as well as saints recognized by the Church like St.
Paul—that I learned why Christians believe the Cross is,
in the phrase of an ancient hymn, *spes unica*, our only hope.
Christ, through suffering in his human nature, took upon
himself all human suffering. He invites us to be joined with
him in baptism because, in the words of Blessed John Paul
II, he "wishes to be united with every individual, and in a
special way he is united with those who suffer."[1]

■ ■ ■

Christ's sufferings, like all his acts, are of infinite value; they have meaning and purpose. The Christian believer's sufferings share in this purpose, for she is, through her baptism, united to Christ. But what of the pain that a Christian carries in her heart from before she was baptized, or before she knew to offer Christ her sufferings?

The beautiful truth is that even past sufferings, in the light of Christ, take on profound meaning, because they are part of the believer who is united to Jesus in the present moment. Here again, as we saw in chapter 1, memory does not have to be the enemy. On the contrary, our healing becomes possible when we admit that our memories are an integral part of who we are. Jesus said, "Those who are well have no need of a physician, but those who are sick" (Mt 9:12). If the Divine Physician is to operate on me, I must have an opening through which he can reach my heart. I must admit that I am wounded, and that my wounds remain. Such a painful admission is yet possible with the aid of God's grace.

At this point, it is important to bring clarity to an area where there has been some controversy among Christian therapists and pastoral counselors: asking Jesus to heal the wounds of past sufferings does *not* require consciously revisiting each of those sufferings.[2] If a disturbing memory does come to mind, I can and should offer it up for healing. However—and I cannot stress this enough—*God's healing power is not limited by our conscious memory.* Our past, whether we remember it or not, is always present to us, because our present identity is formed by our past experiences. For that reason, when God's healing rays reach into our present, they cannot but help suffuse our past as well. Then—over time, and with the help of prayer and the sacraments—when past memories do come up, their sting is softened. We begin to see that even our most painful times contain beauty, inasmuch as they led us—however tangled our path—to our present life in the love of God.

The Mass testifies to how even the most troubling past memories may become the foundation of present grace. In Eucharistic Prayer III, the priest says, "Therefore, O Lord, as we celebrate the memorial of the saving Passion of your Son, his wondrous Resurrection and Ascension into heaven, and as we look forward to his second coming, we offer you in thanksgiving this holy and living sacrifice." To "celebrate the memorial of the saving Passion" means to call it to mind—and calling the Passion to mind means calling to mind images of the darkest hour humanity has ever seen. Yet our memory does not end there; the darkness is followed by the radiance of Jesus' triumphal resurrection and ascension, and by the hope of his second coming. Remember Pope Benedict's great insight: "memory awakens hope" (see chapter 2).

■ ■ ■

We are advised to follow saints' examples, but the dizzying variety of saints can make this a confusing task. As Blessed John XXIII wrote, each saint is "holy in a different way."[3] However, it doesn't take long to discover two things all the saints have in common: They all suffered, and they all experienced joy in the midst of suffering, through their union with Christ.

Among the first saints to testify to such joy was St. Paul, who wrote in his letter to the Colossians, "Now I rejoice in my sufferings for your sake, and in my flesh I complete what is lacking in Christ's afflictions for the sake of his body, that is, the church" (Col 1:24). Paul did not mean that Christ's sufferings were insufficient to redeem humanity; there was nothing "lacking" from them in that sense. Rather, he was demonstrating by example how we, the Church's members, may offer Christ—and, by extension, all the Church—the gift of our own individual suffering within Christ's Mystical Body. Unlike the singular events of the Passion and Resurrection, the member's gift can take place only over the passage of time. Christ is not the richer for it, but it does "complete what is lacking," in that it completes the individual Christian's return to God, which requires that he or she imitate Christ (1 Cor 11:1).

Recall the *Anima Christi* prayer, which pleads, "Within Thy wounds hide me" (see the Reader's Guide on page 185 for the full text). Christ's body is now glorified; it lacks nothing—yet, spiritually speaking, there is room in his Sacred Heart for the Christian to rest (Mt 11:28–30). Likewise, heaven lacks nothing—yet Jesus tells his disciples that it has space for them (Jn 14:2). In each of these cases, the appearance of "lack" is only because God, who is outside of time, has destined in his providence that human beings return to him, in time, through conformity to his Son (Gal 4:19).

Christ has completed his suffering *for* us. But he has not yet completed his suffering *in* us.

■ ■ ■

At times throughout the Church's history, God has granted individual saints the opportunity to "complete what is lacking in Christ's afflictions" not only through their everyday sufferings, but also through experiences that literally imitate the Passion. In the Church's early centuries, saints imitated the crucified Christ through martyrdom—and, like St. Paul, exulted. The account of the martyrdom of Saints Perpetua and Felicity, which took place in a Carthage arena in AD 202, states that, when the crowd demanded they be scourged before a line of gladiators, the saints and their companions "rejoiced at this that they had obtained a share in the Lord's sufferings."[4]

One martyr who obtained an extraordinary share in such sufferings was St. Sebastian. Artists typically depict him shot through with arrows. The image is deceptive, for the assault on him by the Emperor Diocletian's archers is not the most interesting part of his story. The most interesting part is that he survived.

Raised in Milan, Sebastian moved to Rome in about the year 283 so that he might secretly aid the Christians there, who were undergoing fierce persecution at the hands of the state. He became an officer in the imperial guard, a position that enabled him to visit imprisoned Christians who were under the sentence of death and secretly encourage them to stay strong in the faith. In 286, the Emperor Diocletian discovered that Sebastian was a Christian and ordered a squad of archers to execute him. Pierced by numerous arrows, he was left for dead.

Now comes the rest of the story. St. Irene, herself all too familiar with the Romans' persecution of Christians—her husband had been martyred—went out to collect Sebastian's body, and instead found he was still alive. She took him under her wing and he miraculously recovered his health.

Sebastian must have believed God healed him for a purpose. No sooner was he recovered than he placed himself alongside a path where Diocletian would pass, so that he might warn the emperor that his soul was in danger. Shocked to see the man he thought he had killed, Diocletian ordered that Sebastian be clubbed to death. This time, Sebastian did not revive.

Despite Sebastian's heroism, the life of the saint who is known for being "twice martyred" would have little meaning for me were it not for the insights of a Catholic artist and online diarist who was sexually victimized as a young boy. Terry Nelson uses his art and writing to work through his pain, which stems not only from the abuse itself, but also from his family's failure to provide him with protection or understanding. He sees in Sebastian "an allegory for what happens to a person who has been sexually abused in childhood":

> Speaking to a friend who had been abused and degraded as a child, we discussed the issue of identity [and] self-image. . . . My friend is going through great passages of self-knowledge and acceptance, experiencing a wonderful freedom of spirit. At times however, the wounds reopen and she goes through difficult times dealing with the hurt, the pain, and the anger—as well as the lonely sense of isolation that is the result of having one's self-image disfigured by abuse. I mentioned my concept of St. Sebastian, having died in a sense, only to be revived, yet the stigmata of his wounds remaining. . . .
>
> I compared it to the mystery of the saints who actually had the stigmata, which would open and bleed on Fridays and feasts of the Passion. In similar fashion, I believe the person who has been abused, while on the road of recovery, perhaps all of their lives, will

> periodically relive the event with all its pain
> and suffering—only now, like the stigmatist,
> the person may have a better awareness of who
> they are and what happened to them and what
> the pain means. . . . [In this way,] the suffering
> becomes redemptive and healing.[5]

The stigmata he mentions is another literal way in which God enables some saints to attain a deeper union with Christ. Some saints who have the stigmata receive it in the form of actual physical wounds that resemble the five wounds Christ suffered on the Cross, while others receive what is popularly known as "invisible stigmata," feeling the pain of such wounds but without cuts or bleeding. Studying saints who had experiences similar to victims of childhood sexual abuse—particularly those who were physically or psychologically abused in the home—I discovered that a disproportionate number of them were stigmatists. St. Catherine of Siena and St. Gemma Galgani received visible stigmata, while St. Margaret of Cortona, St. Rose of Lima, and St. Margaret Mary Alacoque all received the invisible kind. Each of these holy women was abused in some way as a child by one or more close family members, and each went on to find great joy through suffering in union with Christ. It is as though, even before they received the stigmata, their hearts had already been pierced. What we know of their spiritual journeys suggests that the imprints of the Passion they received—whether visible or invisible—gave new meaning to the sufferings they had already endured.

At the age of eight, Gemma Galgani (1878–1903) underwent the twin traumas of losing her beloved mother to tuberculosis and, as a consequence, being sent by her bereaved father to live temporarily with an aunt. Later in life, writing to her spiritual director, she described her conduct in her aunt's home as "always bad," which (assuming she judged herself accurately) is understandable given how much psychological stress she was under at the time.

As an example of her "bad" behavior, Gemma cited an incident that occurred when her aunt told her to take something over to the aunt's son. The fifteen-year-old boy was seated on his horse as the little girl approached. Gemma relates what happened next:

> When I took [the item] to him, he pinched me, and I gave him so strong a push that he fell down and hurt his head. My aunt tied my hands behind my back for a whole day. I was very angry and told him that I would avenge myself but I did not do so.[6]

Reading her account of the incident, one cannot help but feel for this frail motherless child, separated from her father, treated roughly by a teenage male cousin, and then punished for reacting to the unprovoked physical intrusion. For her to respond with such force as to knock the boy off his horse, she must have felt terribly threatened.

It could be said that Gemma's childhood was longer than the usual one, in that her increasingly fragile health left her in a permanent state of dependence. What comes down to us about her family members suggests that, apart from her parents, many of them treated her with insensitivity and sometimes outright cruelty. Once, when Gemma was about twenty-one, one of her brothers erupted in anger because he wanted to go to the theater and did not have the money. When she tried to calm him, he gave her a black eye.

For the person who lacks familial love, the temptation is to harden one's heart, to develop a shell of cynicism as a means of personal protection. This was not Gemma's way. Under the guidance of grace, her experience of isolation from the love of family led her to seek security in the love of God.

Her stigmata was the answer to a series of prayers she made in which, having been given an extraordinary vision of Jesus bleeding on the Cross, she longed to return his love. She wrote to her spiritual director,

> Two sentiments and two thoughts were born in my heart after the first time Jesus made himself apparent to me and let me see his flowing blood. The first was to love him even to the point of sacrifice. . . . The other thing that was born in my heart, after having seen Jesus, was a great desire to suffer for him, since he had suffered so much for me.[7]

More than two hundred years earlier, in 1674, the French nun St. Margaret Mary Alacoque had a similar vision, awakening in her a like desire to give love for love. In Margaret Mary's own words:

> [Jesus] unfolded to me the inexplicable wounds of his pure love, and to what an excess he had carried it for the love of men, from whom he had received only ingratitude. Our Lord then said "This is much more painful to me than all I suffered in my Passion. If men rendered me some return of love, I should esteem little all I have done for them, and should wish, if such could be, to suffer it over again. But they meet my eager love with coldness and rebuffs."[8]

Jesus ended his message to Margaret Mary with a request: "Do you, at least console and rejoice me by supplying as much as you can for their ingratitude."

I find these last words compelling. Here is a twenty-six-year-old nun, a survivor of childhood trauma, living an utterly obscure life in the silence of the cloister, and now personally given the greatest mission in the world: Love Jesus. As Jesus died for all humanity, this one woman is chosen to be a representative of the countless souls who fail to express the gratitude due to their Redeemer. It is precisely the rejected child whom the Father—through his incarnate Son—most desires to take to his bosom.

■ ■ ■

During the long years of my young adulthood when I was trying, and failing, to believe that God loved me, light finally entered my world one day through the most unexpected means: a work of fiction.

It began in December 1995, when I was a twenty-seven-year-old rock journalist conducting a telephone interview with a Los Angeles rock musician named Ben Eshbach for an online information service (the short-lived *CompuServe WOW!*). Ben's songs contained literary references, so it seemed appropriate to ask what he was reading lately. Both the author and the novel he named were unfamiliar to me—G. K. Chesterton's *The Man Who Was Thursday*—so I decided to track down a copy.

Written in 1907, *The Man Who Was Thursday* begins with an impromptu debate in a London park between two poets. One is a poet of anarchism and revolution. The other calls himself "a poet of law, a poet of order; . . . a poet of respectability." It was easy to choose which character's side to take. I longed to be "creative"—and, like Chesterton's revolutionary poet, I believed creativity was defined by rebellion. For that reason, I strained to be a rebel, wearing the most revealing clothes I could find, peppering my conversation with references to sex, and priding myself on being sexually aggressive. If I could not be truly creative, I could at least be like the post-Madonna pop stars and transvestites whom the media praises for creating themselves.

Looking back, I see that my rebel persona was a lie—a lie I created in an effort to protect myself from the lies imprinted upon my psyche by my abusers. Child sexual abuse thrives upon lies. The abuser lies to the victim, while the victim in turn, trying to cope with her wounds, often finds herself living a lie.

The lies typically begin with the abuser trying to frame the event in the child's mind so that the child thinks she has brought the abuse upon herself. Jesus himself refutes this, condemning the notion that children who are tempted by an adult are in any way responsible for their abuse: "Temptations to sin are sure to come; but woe to him by whom they come!" (Lk 17:1). Woe, that is, not to the one who is tempted, but to the tempter: "It would be better for him if a millstone were hung round his neck and he were cast into the sea, than that he should cause one of these little ones to sin" (Lk 17:2).

Early in his pontificate, Blessed John Paul II echoed Christ's admonition. In a strongly worded message to parents, educators, and mass-media workers, the pope wrote that, "defenseless against the world and adult persons, [children] are naturally ready to accept whatever is offered to them, whether good or bad":

Like soft wax on which every tiniest pressure leaves a mark, so the child is responsive to every stimulus that plays upon his imagination, his emotions, his instincts and his ideas. Yet the impressions received at this age are the ones which are destined to penetrate most deeply into the psychology of the human being and to condition, often in a lasting way, the successive relationship with himself, with others and with his environment. It was precisely out of an intuition regarding the extreme delicacy of this phase of life that pagan wisdom enunciated the well-known pedagogical guideline which direct that *"maxima debetur puero reverentia"* ["the greatest reverence is owed to a child"]; and it is in this same light that we must regard Christ's warning, with its reasoned severity: "Whoever causes one of these little ones who believe in me to sin, it would be better for him to have a great millstone fastened round his neck and to be drowned in the depth of the sea" (Mt 18:6). . . .

The Lord identifies himself with the world of young children. . . . Jesus does not condition children, he does not use children. He calls them, and brings them into his plan for the salvation of the world.[9]

In observing that the impressions received in childhood condition the child's "successive relationship with himself," John Paul addresses another lie spawned by abuse: the denial of the child's identity. When the child is not treated in accordance with his true self—a human being, called by Christ and worthy of reverence—he is vulnerable to developing a false sense of self.

The false self I inhabited during my teens and young adulthood, the sexually aggressive rebel, stemmed from dissociation, a psychological defense mechanism common in trauma victims. My dissociation started with the erroneous belief that I was responsible for my abuse. Feeling responsible, I felt tainted. Feeling tainted, I felt inferior. Feeling inferior, I wanted to regain a sense of control over my life.

That was why I mentally dissociated myself from my victim identity in favor of a persona in which I could feel powerful. Since my greatest vulnerability was in the sexual realm, I chose to announce—through provocative dress, language, and behavior—that I was master of my own sexuality. Beneath the posturing, however, remained the soul of a little girl desperate to be told she was valued not for what she did, but for who she was.

■ ■ ■

So, reading *The Man Who Was Thursday*, I rooted for the revolutionary—until a line spoken by his adversary jumped out at me. In response to the revolutionary's claim that "the poet delights in disorder only," the "poet of order" insists to the contrary: "The most poetical thing in the world is not being sick."

The words were meant to be shocking, and they were—shocking enough to force me to pause and let a sliver of grace's light enter in. At that moment, I desired with all my heart to experience healing, to have my life ordered from the top down, to know the *poetry* of not being sick.

It would take another four years and a lot more Chesterton before the grace that had begun working in me would bring me to conversion. In the meantime, I saw a psychiatrist, as I had done for years. Unfortunately, however, as often happens with victims of traumatic stress, my condition was misdiagnosed. Because my moods swung between relative stability and suicidal despair, I was judged to have cyclical depression.

When, in 1999, at thirty-one, I finally entered into the light of Christian faith, the most dramatic evidence of my conversion was that my despair disappeared. The influx of divine grace into my soul gave me the certain knowledge that God existed and that he cared about me. That was enough to banish all hopelessness; I vowed never again to entertain thoughts of self-harm. The following year, I discontinued therapy; there seemed no need to keep it up, given that I no longer had depressive symptoms.

However, as I adjusted to the life of grace, I found my healing was not as complete as I had thought. Although the freedom from the temptation to self-harm seemed indeed permanent, anxiety remained, sometimes plaguing me for weeks or months at a time.

When the stress became too much to bear, I sought therapy again—this time with a Catholic therapist—and began to come to terms with the reality of having undergone childhood sexual abuse. That led to my finally being diagnosed in 2007 with post-traumatic stress disorder— after living with the symptoms for a quarter-century. (Most trauma victims do not develop full-blown PTSD, but more than 80 percent of victims of childhood sexual abuse will experience some symptoms of the disorder.[10])

Until receiving the diagnosis, I did not realize that the unnerving emotional responses that hit me a few times a year and had plagued me frequently during my youth were flashbacks. I thought that flashbacks entailed a complete loss of touch with reality. My psychiatrist explained to me that some PTSD sufferers endure emotional flashbacks, where they maintain contact with the present while emotionally regressing to a past experience of trauma.

Learning the name for what I suffered gave me relief from the strain of uncertainty; that, in turn, caused some of my symptoms to diminish. A year later, however, my PTSD reared up with a vengeance in the most unexpected of places: the Catholic theological school where I was surrounded by kind and prayerful people.

■ ■ ■

The thought of going back to school had been on my mind for some time, but fear of failure kept me from making the leap. What changed my mind was reading an essay by Fr. Peter F. Ryan, S.J., on discerning the elements of one's personal vocation. He wrote, "[With] respect to future possibilities, we cannot discern whether we should *do* something, but only whether we should *try* to do it. . . . God calls us only to try."[11]

Fr. Ryan's advice proved life-altering: I earned my master's degree in theology from a pontifically licensed school, and am now continuing my studies there en route to a doctorate. However, my first year at the school was harrowing at times—not because of any lack of generosity on the part of the faculty or students, but because studying exacerbated my post-traumatic stress.

Not knowing why my classes revived the old feeling of being on edge, I thought at first that it had to do with the tension of being surrounded by celibates. Nearly all my professors were priests, and 90 percent of my classmates were young men studying for the priesthood. As a convert to Catholicism whose earlier life choices were less than admirable, and particularly as a survivor of sexual abuse, I had deep-seated insecurities related to my past. Being in an atmosphere of men who were, to my imagination, "pure" made me conscious of my own guilt. Moreover, having memories of growing up in what I remember as a sexually porous environment where I was exposed to adults' nudity and sex talk on a daily basis, I had the feeling of being sexually miscalibrated. My greatest fear was that I might inadvertently respond to one of my professors or classmates in a sexually inappropriate manner, such as making an innuendo or staring at someone for too long. Such interactions could pass without comment in a traditional university environment but would certainly be noticed at a Catholic seminary.

By the spring semester, my self-consciousness had eased. Professors and classmates had grown familiar, seeming less like supernaturally pure beings and more like ordinary men called to an extraordinary path of perfection. However, my emotional tension continued, and in fact got worse. With a stamina that seemed miraculous, I managed to stay calm in class, but as soon as I crossed the street to get lunch from the cafeteria at a neighboring university, my tears would flow.

What was wrong with me? I would find out one afternoon through a flashback—not just an emotional one, but one that made reality momentarily disappear.

I felt it coming on during my history class. The professor was talking about Philip of Hesse, a German ruler who successfully pressured Martin Luther to condone his taking a second wife while still married to his first one. Philip, the professor explained, claimed it was necessary for him to take a second wife because he was unable to control himself sexually.

There was nothing prurient about the way the professor told the story—no smirking, winking, joking, or unnecessary sexual details. His tone was as serious as when he discussed the Hundred Years' War. Yet, at the moment he mentioned Philip's lack of sexual self-control, I felt a violent flashback coming on.

Why now? I thought—but could not spare the brainpower to figure it out. All my mental energy had to go toward coping with the looming threat of tears. I glanced over at the door. All I had to do was get up and dash five feet and I could be in the hall, five more feet and I would be in the ladies' room. But then I would miss the rest of class, and I had already used up my absences for the semester.

If I can just hold it back, I can make it through . . . My cheeks flushed. I took a breath and lifted my right hand to my forehead, pretending to be battling a headache as I wiped my eyes. If the professor noticed anything, he didn't show it; he continued his lecture, while I recovered sufficiently to absorb myself in taking notes.

Two hours later, I stood on the Metro platform, waiting for the subway that would take me home, and feeling strange. There was that sense of being on edge, but also something more. My mind felt like a file cabinet with one file out of place. Something had happened that I had not fully processed.

Taking out my notebook, I began journaling in an effort to retrace my steps. The first thing that came to mind was the taxi ride I had taken to school, having missed my morning train. Then, in history class—

Suddenly, for a split second, I wasn't on the platform anymore. I was six or seven years old, sitting in my little Alice in Wonderland dress on the faded green wall-to-wall carpet in my mother's bedroom. My mother had taken a file out of her ancient portable metal file cabinet and pulled from it a sheet of onionskin paper on which were typed some uneven lines. She was reading to me from it, declaiming in dramatic fashion—or was she? Perhaps she had only given me the poem to read, and I was imagining her voice in my mind as I perused its short verses.

I returned to reality with a jolt. When you see a toddler undergo an injury, there is one brief, disturbing moment when he is dead silent—then his mouth opens in a wail. Likewise, I was frozen for a moment as I regained my orientation on the Metro platform. The front light of a train was visible in the distance, making its inexorable approach. With commuters around, I couldn't wail, but the tears started streaming down.

What I had flashed back to was the afternoon that my mother induced me to read her poetry. She had taken up the art during her separation from my father, when she was exploring new ways to express herself. The poem (which my mother doesn't recall having written) stuck out in my memory because I didn't understand it and needed my mother to explain it. It used obscene street slang to describe a certain practice of male prisoners who were unable to control themselves sexually.

The tears flowed freely as I rode the Metro, while my fellow commuters pretended not to notice. Yet, even as the pain of the memory burned, there was a feeling of relief and a kind of freedom. *No wonder I've been feeling so wounded*, I thought. *I am wounded. I have nothing to be ashamed of.*

Still more liberating was the insight of why the flashback began when and where it did. The key, I realized, was memory. In my history class, more than in any other course I was taking, I had to mentally store factoids on a variety of levels—information such as who said what to whom, where they said it, and why. Moreover, to do well on the tests, not only did I have to recall individual names, dates, and places, but I also had to identify the causal links between events occurring in different countries at different times. My memory was facing demands unlike any it had faced since childhood. Naturally, the need to make new connections would cause neural pathways to form where they had not formed in years—and perhaps hit the landmines of long-suppressed memories in the process.

This insight did not alter my vulnerability to flashbacks. What it did change, as I pondered it over time, was my *fear* of them. I realized that the most important thing in my study life at that time was to follow my "vocation to try" (to use Fr. Ryan's phrase). If God was truly calling me to study—and I believed he was—then he wanted me to *try* to absorb what was being taught in class, even if doing so had painful side effects. Offered up to God, my symptoms of post-traumatic stress would no longer be purposeless pain. They would become a sacrifice.

■ ■ ■

An essential part of every saint's biography is her manner of death. How a saint dies reflects the depth to which she experiences the Passion in her own flesh. So I find it particularly meaningful that both St. Josephine Bakhita and St. Gemma Galgani, when at death's door, endured flashbacks to the most painful moments of their lives.

Bakhita, in her final agony, relived the horrors of slavery, begging her nurse, "Please, loosen the chains . . . they are heavy!" But just before she passed away her countenance changed into a radiant smile. Mary had come to free her. Bakhita's last words were "Our Lady! Our Lady!"

Gemma, during the course of her twenty-five years, had experienced the most excruciating pain due to illness—and this in addition to the pain she joyfully suffered from her stigmata. Yet as she lay dying, the episode that flashed before her was not one of physical suffering, but of emotional suffering. She was mentally transported six years back in time, to when she was nineteen and her father had just died. Her family home was invaded by creditors who closed her father's pharmacy, seized what little furniture remained, and dumped out Gemma's purse to snatch the two lire that were all she had to her name.

Her body, which had borne the marks of Christ's suffering so many times over the course of her brief adult life, did not have stigmata on her deathbed. Gemma's flashbacks were like a final stigmata. Like Bakhita, she too, after returning from her flashback, left this world bearing a peaceful smile.

■ ■ ■

As I learn how to recognize potential triggers, my flashbacks are becoming fewer and farther between. Still, every so often, I receive a reminder of my vulnerability. The last was three months ago, as I write, and it was again at school—but this time it was different.

Making small talk with a faculty member one afternoon after class, I said something I thought was perfectly innocuous—but it seemed to offend. The reaction was sudden; the faculty member's face darkened, and he had nothing more to say. He gave no indication why he found my words offensive, and I was too embarrassed to ask, so I quickly excused myself and made my escape down the stairs.

Normally I am comfortable conversing with someone who has authority over me; I can cope when someone reacts negatively to me; and I can tolerate someone who inexplicably alters his demeanor. But put them all together and it is the perfect storm.

At the bottom of the stairs, my heart racing, I faced a choice. To my right was the library. If I went there, I might be able to distract myself, hold back the flashback as best I could, get some schoolwork done—and suffer on my way home.

To my left was the chapel. If I went there, there was no telling how long I would cry and who might see me.

With a push, perhaps, from my guardian angel, I turned left.

Finding a seat in the back of the chapel, I sank to my knees. There was one other person there, a seminarian, some distance away, so I began to let the tears out as quietly as I could.

Ahead of me, at the front of the church, I could see the faint light of the tabernacle lamp—the sign of our Lord's presence in the Blessed Sacrament. A pleasant image from my childhood flashed before me for a moment as I remembered the *ner tamid*, the "eternal light" that hangs before the ark of every synagogue.

As the tears started to flow, I whispered, "Dear Jesus, I know I can choose to suffer this with you, or without you. I choose to suffer this *with* you. Don't leave me."

I cried and cried, and worried that I was being heard; gave up worrying, and cried some more, until the fight-or-flight hormones rushing through my system finally dissipated. Yet, upon rising, even as some leftover tears trickled out, I felt different from other times I had suffered flashbacks. For the first time, I felt that, even in my most intimate suffering, I was not alone. In the ancient phrase quoted by Pope Benedict, "God cannot suffer, but he can *suffer with*."[12]

When I finally made it back out the chapel door, I could not tell whether those last drops were tears of sorrow, or of joy. Perhaps they were both.

CHAPTER 4

The Love That Transforms

Learning the true meaning of spiritual childhood with St. Thérèse of Lisieux

> There was a little flower garden with painted wooden palings in front of it; close by was a ditch, on its fresh green bank grew a little daisy; the sun shone as warmly and brightly upon it as on the magnificent garden flowers, and therefore it thrived well. One morning it had quite opened, and its little snow-white petals stood round the yellow center, like the rays of the sun. It did not mind that nobody saw it in the grass, and that it was a poor despised flower; on the contrary, it was quite happy, and turned towards the sun, looking upward and listening to the song of the lark high up in the air.
>
> — Hans Christian Andersen
> "The Daisy"

I had seen many strange things in my thirteen years, but the object before my eyes one afternoon in 1982 had to be one of the strangest: an ornately decorated gift box enshrining a minuscule part of the body of a woman who had been dead for eighty-five years.

The box lay atop the bureau of my best friend Stephanie, whose father had brought it to her from Rome as a Confirmation gift. It contained a relic of the Carmelite nun she had chosen as her Confirmation saint, Thérèse of Lisieux, though Stephanie spelled her Confirmation name like Thérèse's namesake, Teresa of Avila.

Since the day we first encountered each other at lunch in our middle school's cafeteria, Stephanie and I knew we were soul sisters—born on the very same day, just hours apart. Given that she and I had determined to be alike in as many things as possible, to look at her exotic gift box and learn what it contained was for me a strange reminder of our differences in background. In my family, we cherished some keepsakes that had belonged to deceased relatives, but we never would have imagined keeping fragments of the relatives themselves, let alone someone of no relation at all.

Stephanie clearly felt that the relic, encased in a plastic pendant, was something special, though she couldn't explain to me exactly why. After she let me satisfy my curiosity by examining it, we turned the conversation to her Confirmation name. That too was a novelty for me. The previous year, I had received many gifts in honor of my bat mitzvah, but nothing so grand as a new addition to my initials.

"So now you're Stephanie Suzanne Teresa Wimmer," I mused. "S.S.T.W."

Stephanie smiled. "My aunt says it stands for"—and here she broke into laughter—"Super Sonic Transporter Woman!"

I cracked up too. Stephanie's laugh was one of the most adorable things about her. Nearly an octave below her normal speaking voice, it would emerge like a wave of gasps from deep within her gut. Few could hear it without dissolving into laughter themselves. Sometimes her friends, hearing it in the school cafeteria, would try in good fun to imitate it, which of course made Stephanie laugh even harder. I didn't know it at the time, but the unself-conscious way she had of abandoning herself to the joy of the present moment was a gift she shared with her heavenly patron.

■ ■ ■

The word *relic* comes from the Latin *reliquiae,* for the noun "remains," which in turn comes from the verb *reliquere,* "to leave behind." It makes a peculiar kind of sense, because in order to leave something behind, you have to go somewhere. So a saint's relics are what was "left behind" on earth when the saint's soul made its journey to heaven.

At the same time, the Church's veneration of relics reflects its belief that "[man], though made of body and soul, is a unity."[1] Although presently the souls of those who have died exist apart from their bodies, such separation is not natural, and it will not go on forever. In the words of the *Catechism,* "The human body shares in the dignity of 'the image of God': it is a human body precisely because it is animated by a spiritual soul, and it is the whole human person that is intended to become, in the body of Christ, a temple of the Spirit. . . . [The soul] does not perish when it separates from the body at death, and it will be reunited with the body at the final Resurrection" (*CCC* 364, 366).

From the earliest days of the Church, Christians defended the unity of body and soul against heretical sects that argued for dualism—the belief that body and soul are completely separate. These sects, which included the Manicheans and the Gnostics, held that matter was inherently evil; therefore, it was not in the soul's nature to be associated with a body. In their view, the body was a mere instrument, to be used and ultimately discarded. Against their errors, the Church, speaking through teachers such as St. Augustine—a onetime Manichean who converted to Christianity—upheld the fundamental goodness of creation. Original sin wounded this goodness, but did not destroy it.

The dualist heresy still thrives today, particularly among atheists and those who call themselves "spiritual but not religious." The "spiritual but not religious" believe, like the Gnostics, that their body exists only as a shell to be transcended. Atheists go further and propound a philosophy called materialism—the idea that the human person is just a collection of chemicals, without a spiritual element.

My friend Colin, a fellow survivor of childhood sexual abuse, entertained materialistic views while studying René Descartes in college. Suffering from depression and self-medicating with alcohol, he was far from the Catholic faith of his childhood. He writes of his mindset during that dark time:

> My Gnostic-Manichean tendencies . . . throughout my life have frequently led me to take a dualistic view of myself, in which the "real" me is the mental or spiritual me, while my body is the shell in which "I" reside. At most, I tended to view "myself" as being confined to

> my head, with the rest of the body acting as a
> sort of mechanical apparatus for transporting
> me around and dogging me with persistent
> appetites.[2]

Colin aptly describes one of the biggest blind spots of materialist philosophy. By denying any actuality to the spiritual part of the human person, materialists are at a loss to explain the mystery of human consciousness—how one collection of chemicals can be aware that it is different from another. To the materialist, when it comes to individual identity, there is no "there" there; no real "I" writing this book, and no real "you" reading it. (This belief does not, alas, prevent materialists from attempting to write bestsellers.)

It is the way we know and experience things, then, that gives the lie to the materialist. In each person, intellect, understanding, and will do not exist in a vacuum; they are *embodied*. When I am standing in a crowded subway car and someone steps on my toe, I know that it is *my* toe that was stepped on, because I feel the pain. Somebody didn't just step on my toe; they stepped on *me*. At the same time, I am conscious that the person who stepped on my toe is someone who is *not* me. If my soul only happened to be connected with my body, and was not united with it in the deepest, innermost way, how would I know I was separate from anyone else? How would I feel an attack on my body as being an attack on myself? It is my basic human experience of the reality of my own unity of body and soul that enables me to function as a human being and have relationships with others.

When we recognize the unity of body and soul as being fundamental to human nature, we receive another insight into why the Church venerates saints' relics. They remind us of the general resurrection that is to come on the last day, when, in each resurrected believer, the glory of the soul will overflow into the body.[3]

Colin returned to the Church during his late twenties and found comfort in its understanding "that we are incarnate beings, that our bodies are as much ourselves as our minds are."[4] He also found, to his delight, that traditional artistic depictions of saints reflect this understanding of the body, sometimes in surprising ways. For example,

> The icon of St. Denis depicts halos around both his severed head and over the stump on his body where the head was formerly attached, as if to reiterate the theological truth that the bishop-martyr of Paris was not only holy in mind and spirit, but in body as well. It is this particularly Catholic reference back to the body that might lead others to think of us as having a taste for the macabre, with our relics . . . and our crucifixes, which starkly depict the Man who gave himself over to death for the forgiveness of sins. We need constant reminders that our humanity entails being embodied, that our bodies are ourselves, and not merely our possessions to do with as we please.[5]

■ ■ ■

The souls of the saints in heaven await the day they will be reunited with their bodies, and yet are in perfect bliss.[6] Having God, they feel no lack. Here on earth, however, one's happiness and holiness entail being mindful of the integral connection between body and soul. If I try to impede the unity of body and soul, I can cause myself the deepest harm.

Knowing this gives me insight into the turmoil I underwent during the years when, suffering from dissociation, I committed acts of self-harm in private and put on a false persona in public (see chapters 1 and 3). As I noted earlier, my desire to cut myself stemmed from the desire to get my mind off my mental pain. I thought that because I felt such violence in my soul, the right thing to do was to bring it out into my body. The urge to self-harm was in this sense a kind of twisted recognition that my soul and body were out of sync. But it was indeed twisted, because in any situation—whether personal or communal—the answer to violence is never violence. It is peace. What I truly needed was not to rile my body, but to quiet my soul.

The same was true when, wishing to escape my identity as an abuse victim, I tried to create an alternate persona. Again, my subconscious desire was to correct a painful dichotomy between how I felt on the inside and how I was on the outside. Again, I reacted by bringing my imbalance outward, when the most healing thing would have been to bring balance inward.

Now that I know my identity is to be found in Christ, I realize the importance of avoiding acting from my pathology. But there remains the challenge of learning how to act from my *wellness*, for my wellness coexists with my wounds.

As I write, I am taken back to a moment when I was four-and-a-half years old. I was born with strabismus, a vision disorder that made me cross-eyed. When I was just one year old, my parents arranged for me to have a corrective operation. I am forever grateful to them for getting

me the care I needed, for without it I would have become
blind. However, the result was only a partial success; my
eyes were no longer crossed, but my left eye's muscles
remained weak. As a result, I developed strabismic amblyopia, which made my left eye look "lazy."

The interesting thing about strabismic amblyopia
is that the condition originates not in the eye itself, but,
rather, in the brain's attempt to compensate for the strabismus. In childhood strabismus, the child's brain receives
misaligned images from her eyes. The brain's subconscious
defense is to tune out the image from the weaker eye—
suppressing it in favor of the stronger eye's image. This
results in strabismic amblyopia, as the eye whose image is
suppressed becomes the "lazy eye." If it is not corrected by
the time the child is ten years old, it can result in permanent visual loss, as the child's brain becomes habituated
to suppressing the lazy eye.

By the time I was four-and-a-half, it was clear that I
would need a second eye operation. The ophthalmolo-
gist told my parents that, before the procedure could
take place, I would need to wear an eye patch for several
months, alternating each day between one eye and the
other, to build up my muscles. This strategy was intended
to break my brain's habit of suppression, so that the operation would have a better chance of success. So that I would
not look like a pirate, my parents opted to have me wear a
disposable adhesive patch—essentially a large eye-shaped
Band-Aid.

Need I say I *hated* the patch? Any four-year-old would,
but I especially detested it because, by then, I was just
beginning to read, and my passion was comic strips. And
so, the image that comes to me right now is of my having

just come home after a day at pre-kindergarten, with the patch over my dominant (right) eye. Mom is not paying attention to me because she is engrossed in a boring TV program called *Watergate*, which is being broadcast live on all three networks. Realizing an opportunity, I grab the comics section of today's newspaper from the kitchen table. Then I sneak off to my bedroom, close the door, lie on my stomach atop my bedspread, and carefully peel off the corner of the patch from my right eye, to better read what Peppermint Patty is saying to Charlie Brown. I know that what I am doing is wrong, but the temptation is too great. It is so much easier to read with my strong eye than with the weak one, the eye that must be strengthened if I am to preserve my sight.

Looking back, I see the temptation to remove the patch as akin to the temptation to act from my pathology. When I illicitly used my right eye to read the comics, I was, in effect, tuning out—suppressing a weak but vital part of myself. In the immediate moment, my secret rebellion enabled me to read more easily, but it ultimately put my vision at grave risk. Likewise, acting from my pathology may, in the immediate moment, appear to save me pain and discomfort, but it ultimately leads to moral blindness.

Acting from my wellness is like trying to read with my weak eye. I can see well enough to pursue my goal, but it requires great persistence, as my mind—so used to tuning out and suppressing—is yet in need of healing. But if I don't get discouraged, then, given time and God's continued grace, I will see rightly for I will see the truth and live in the truth. "The eye is the lamp of the body. So, if your eye is sound, your whole body will be full of light" (Mt 6:22).

How then do I take the first step? How do I find strength when all I have to work with is weakness? When painful memories trigger physical reactions, how do I progress, like St. Paul, from the despair of inhabiting a "body of death" (Rom 7:24) to the hope of walking "according to the spirit" (Rom 8:4)? How do I become a fully integrated human being?

The answers to these questions lie in two great books: the book of sacred scripture and, in scripture's light, the book of nature—specifically human nature, created in the image of God. The book of nature reaches us in its fullest glory in the lives of the saints. In manifesting God's design for humanity's total vocation, the saints show us what it means to be fully human.[7]

I think of sacred scripture as being like a globe showing a detailed political map of the world—where the countries and cities are, where the major roads are, and so on. If I study it, I will know what is my destination—heaven—and what I need to do in order to get there. The saints' lives are like that same globe, but with a new dimension—a *topographic* globe, revealing not only the path I must take, but also what peaks and valleys I can expect along the way. Discovering that weak human beings like myself have reached heaven after crossing the most tortuous terrain, I have confidence that I too can do so with God's grace, no matter how trying my journey.

If, then, I seek to learn what it means to be comfortable in my own skin, I need to find a saint who learned to be comfortable in her own skin, and follow her example. The most helpful example would be one who was naturally weak, fearful, and fragmented, who grew in grace to become strong, courageous, and integrated. No one better fits the bill than Thérèse of Lisieux, who insisted that she was not a great soul but "a very *small* and very imperfect one."[8]

■ ■ ■

Most of what we know of St. Thérèse (1873–1897), a nun of the Carmelite convent at Lisieux, France, is from *The Story of a Soul*, a collection of autobiographical writings. In 1895, Thérèse began the work in obedience to an order given by the prioress of her community, Mother Agnes, who happened to be her real-life sister Pauline. Mother Agnes had enjoyed hearing Thérèse speak of her childhood memories and wanted to have a permanent record of them.

Thérèse, although only twenty-two, was already well advanced on the path to holiness at the time she began her autobiography. She saw her sister's order as an opportunity to "begin to sing what I must sing eternally: 'The Mercies of the Lord.'"[9]

With those words, Thérèse shows us the proper role of memory. Memory is not to be feared; it is to be purified in the white heat of divine love. As divine love's light enters into the wounds left by past sorrows, we come to realize how the divine mercy carried us even during the times of our lives when we felt abandoned by God.

That is why, in the opening pages of her autobiography, Thérèse stresses that she is thankful for the gift of remembrance: "God granted me the favor of opening my intelligence at an early age and of imprinting childhood recollections so deeply on my memory that it seems the things I'm about to recount happened only yesterday."[10] Her memories were inseparable from her gratitude for divine providence. All the things that had happened to her, whether pleasurable or painful at the time, were now visible to her only through the light of God's loving plan for her life. This is a saint who, even while enduring the most intense physical sufferings on her deathbed, was able to say, "everything is a grace" and really mean it.[11]

As she continues her story, it seems Thérèse stresses her gratitude partly to steel the reader for the many childhood sufferings she will recount. One could say, in a sense, that she sees her life as the story of a soul who went from suffering without God to suffering *with* God.

Of course, as Thérèse would be the first to say, God is never truly absent from us. However, we can will to deny him entrance into our heart. When we hold onto resentment that our own will is not being done, we become locked in a solitary prison of self-pity. Thérèse herself experienced the interior pain of this prison. The key that freed her is what she wants to share with us: the realization that, to the degree that we can say "Not my will, but thy will be done," suffering can become the foundation for a closer union with God. Thérèse spoke of this during her final illness: "I have suffered very much since I have been on earth, but, if in my childhood I suffered with sadness, it is no longer the way I suffer. It is with joy and peace."[12]

In *The Story of a Soul*, Thérèse, the youngest of five sisters, illustrates this truth by means of a childhood recollection. One day, when she was about three, her sister Léonie decided to divest herself of her doll, its dresses, and the fragments of fabric she had saved for making doll clothes, putting them all into a basket. Bringing the basket to Thérèse and another sister, Céline, Léonie said, "Here, my little sisters, *choose*. I'm giving you all this." Céline reached in first and took a ball of wool. Thérèse thought for a moment, then reached out and said, "I choose all!" Without any complaint from Céline, she simply took the whole basket.

> This little incident of my childhood is a summary of my whole life; later on, when perfection [in holiness] was set before me, I understood that to become *a saint* one had to suffer much, seek out always the most perfect thing to do, and forget self. I understood, too, there were many degrees of perfection and each soul was free to respond to the advances of our Lord, to do little or much for him, in a word, to *choose* among the sacrifices he was asking. Then, as in the days of my childhood, I cried out, "My God, *'I choose all!'* I don't want to be a *saint by halves*, I'm not afraid to suffer for you, I fear only one thing, to keep my *own will*; so take it, for *'I choose all'* that you will![13]

Thérèse's parents, Louis Martin and Zélie Guérin, were exceptionally holy—so much so that they are presently on their way to becoming canonized saints, having been beatified by Pope Benedict XVI. However, even the most perfect parents cannot ensure that their children's youth will pass without troubles. Thérèse was only four and a half when her mother's death from breast cancer sent her into a "winter of trial."[14]

Normally, Thérèse, as the youngest child, was always under the protective eye of one of her parents or sisters. Not so in the hours following her mother's death: "No one had any time to pay any attention to me, and I saw many things they would have hidden from me."[15] Her next words are remarkable for what they reveal about her purification of memory:

> For instance, once I was standing before the lid of the coffin which had been placed upright in the hall. I stopped for a long time gazing at it. Though I'd never seen one before, I understood what it was. I was so little that in spite of Mamma's short stature, I had to *raise* my head to take in its full height. It appeared *large* and *dismal*.
>
> Fifteen years later, I was to stand before another coffin, [Lisieux Carmel convent foundress] Mother Geneviève's. It was similar in size. I imagined myself back once again in the days of my childhood and all those memories flooded into my mind. True, it was the same Thérèse who looked, but she'd *grown up* and the coffin appeared *smaller*. I had no need to *raise* my head to see and, in fact, no longer *raised* it but to contemplate *heaven*, which to me was *filled with joy*. All my trials had come to an end and the winter of my soul had passed on forever.[16]

These paragraphs encapsulate Thérèse's journey from suffering in "sadness" to suffering in "joy and peace."[17] Perhaps most striking is her acknowledgment that Mother Geneviève's coffin was a memory trigger. Had she allowed herself to be carried away by the images it evoked, she could have suffered a painful flashback, reliving the experience of being a devastated little girl. Instead, we see that even as her childhood trauma comes to mind, she remains grounded in the present.

Note especially how she refuses to dissociate from her childhood self. "It was the same Thérèse who looked." The traumatized child is perfectly integrated into the woman who has "*grown up*." Thérèse's present joy in contemplating heaven comes not in spite of remembering her trauma, but *because* of it. It is precisely because the Little Flower experienced "winter" that she now raises her head in gratitude for the spring.

■ ■ ■

What had changed since Thérèse's childhood that enabled her to accept suffering in the love of Christ? Thérèse tells us she grew up in a single moment, in the early morning of December 25, 1886. She calls it her "Christmas conversion," because, even though she had always had faith, the graces she received completely transformed her understanding of her identity in Christ.

Thérèse was nearly fourteen years old, but was emotionally much younger. Still bereft from her mother's death, she was also pained at being separated from two of her sisters, Pauline and Marie, who had entered the Carmel Lisieux. She "didn't do any housework whatsoever," and was given to crying jags. "I was really unbearable because of my extreme touchiness."[18]

On that Christmas morning, arriving home from Midnight Mass with her father and sister Céline, Thérèse put out her shoes by the fireplace. For years, it had been a family tradition for her father to fill the children's "magic shoes" like Christmas stockings. Thérèse was the only child who continued to put out her shoes, for she eagerly looked forward to the annual ritual even though she was well beyond the age of believing in such "magic."

Louis Martin, however, after the late Mass, had little energy left to play Santa Claus. As Thérèse ascended the stairs, she overheard him say with exasperation, "Well, fortunately this will be the last year!"[19]

The words pierced Thérèse's heart. She froze, and the tears started to well up. But then something happened— something completely unexpected. She received, in her own words, "the grace of leaving my childhood": "I felt *charity* enter into my soul, and the need to forget myself and to please others."[20]

The first thing she did was to quickly come back downstairs and show her father—who was worried as he realized she had heard him—that she was not at all offended. Joyfully, she examined the gifts that had been placed in her shoes, to her father's delighted relief. But this grace of desiring to forget her self-interest for others' sake did not end with her family; she felt at the same time "a great desire to work for the conversion of sinners."[21] It would ultimately lead her to follow her sisters into Carmel, where she would offer up all that she was and all that she had, for the salvation of the world.

Thérèse's Christmas conversion was the beginning of her "Little Way"—the practice of spiritual childhood, which she would develop and perfect at Carmel, under the guidance of sacred scripture. At its root, the Little Way entails a *continuous* conversion in the sense of the Latin root *convertere*, to turn around.

Forms of the word *convertere* appear throughout the Vulgate, St. Jerome's foundational Latin translation of the Bible. Most often, they appear in the cry of the believer begging for the grace of conversion of heart: "Restore [*converte*] us, O God; let thy face shine, that we may be saved!" (Ps 80:3). "Bring [*converte*] me back that I may be restored, for thou art the Lord my God" (Jer 31:18).

"Restore [*converte*] us to thyself, O LORD, that we may be restored" (Lam 5:21).

The key to remaining, like Thérèse, a child before God is to seek God's grace at every moment, so that we may always be converted—turned toward him. I think of it this way: When a little girl is walking with her father, she becomes distraught if her father lets her run so far ahead that when she finally turns to look for him, she cannot see where he has gone. On the other hand, if her father, seeing her run ahead of him, stops her, turns her back around, and insists she stay at his side, the little girl will briefly experience the humiliation of being corrected. Yet her humiliation turns to joy when she realizes her father is correcting her out of love, for she is safe only when she remains by his side.

Upon her Christmas conversion, Thérèse, while being emotionally "grown up," became like that little girl before God, experiencing simultaneous humiliation and conversion at every moment for the rest of her life. The holier she became, the more sensitive she became to her natural inclination to run ahead of God, preferring her own will to his. Every time she caught herself doing this, she immediately sought the grace to turn back to him—a grace she knew "God never refuses."[22] That is why, in her final illness, she was able to say, "I experience a living joy not only when I discover I'm imperfect, but especially when I feel I am."[23] In her heart, it was always Christmas.

■ ■ ■

My friend Stephanie and I remained close through high school, but drifted apart when her college plans took her to a distant part of the country. After college, when we were both living in New Jersey and working in New York City, we got together from time to time, but it was not the same. She was as kind and good-humored as ever, but I was suffering from depression and failed to keep up my end of the friendship.

Yet, even when I had seemingly forgotten about Stephanie, she never forgot about me. Years after I last saw her, I began to keep an online journal. She found my site in about 2005 and began to leave friendly comments. I commented back, but did not reach out further. The reason was no longer depression. I was preparing to enter the Catholic Church and, being taken up with my new faith, sought the company of fellow Christians. Although Stephanie was baptized, confirmed, and married in the Church, she was not interested in religion, so I felt we had little left in common. When preparing to move to Washington, DC, in July 2007, I did not think of inviting her to my going-away party.

Then came the day later that year, just after Christmas, when I really needed a friend. A call came in from my endocrinologist's office with the results of a biopsy of a lump on my thyroid gland. I had not been worried about the test, because the lump had previously been biopsied and was benign. This time, however, the results were not so good: "suspicious for papillary carcinoma."

It was shocking to be faced with the possibility of a deadly disease when I was only thirty-nine. Distressed, I posted a prayer request on my blog, writing plaintively, "Nobody in my family has ever had anything like this so young." Almost immediately, an e-mail arrived with the header, "Hi Dawn, I have advanced thyroid cancer." My heart sank when I saw that the sufferer was my childhood soul sister—Stephanie.

After giving a rundown of her own illness, Stephanie provided extraordinarily detailed advice on thyroid-cancer treatment. It was exactly the kind of information I needed at that moment, when I was feeling frightened and helpless.

Stephanie had then been battling the disease for more than four years. She was diagnosed with it two weeks before her wedding.

I wrote back to thank her for her advice and concern, and we began enjoying our first correspondence in more than a decade. Her next message, recounting an exchange with her husband Tom, showed that her love of laughter remained as I remembered it from eighth grade:

> Right after my biopsy this past April, I was having double vision, because the tumor was inflamed and pressing on my optic nerves. So, to the tune of a New Order song (I don't remember the name, but the lyric is "Oh you have green eyes, oh you have gray eyes, oh you have blue eyes"), Tom started to sing, "Oh you have one eye, oh you have two eyes, oh you have three eyes," and I could not stop laughing. Even when they were making the mask needed for my radiation treatment, I couldn't stop laughing and I think I annoyed the techs a little bit. I do have two tiny little dots tattooed on either side of my face, which I kind of take as tiny badges of honor now.

When Stephanie's Confirmation saint Thérèse was dying of tuberculosis, Sr. Marie of the Eucharist—one of

Thérèse's sisters with her at Carmel—wrote of her in a letter: "With regard to her morale, it's always the same: she is gaiety itself, she makes everyone who comes near her laugh. . . . I believe she'll die laughing because she is so happy."[24]

One month after the biopsy, I went into the hospital to have the lump removed from my thyroid. As I recovered at home and awaited the pathology results, Stephanie wrote to me, "I have this strong gut feeling you do not have cancer—I have this feeling I somehow took the bullet, so to speak, for both of us,"—here she typed a smiley face—" and out of my journey thus far, oh boy, I do have some amusing stories!"

St. Thérèse wrote, "I have the vocation of a warrior."[25] In her final weeks, she said, "I keep nothing in my hands. Everything I have, everything I merit, is for the Church and for souls."[26]

As it turned out, I did have cancer—but mine, unlike Stephanie's, did not spread. After one more operation to remove the rest of my thyroid, I made a perfect recovery. Stephanie did take the bullet for me—at least, she willed to do so. I have no doubt that God will reward her desire to make that gift of self, which made her ever more like her heavenly patron.

"Thérèse," says Pope Benedict, "points out to us all that Christian life consists in living to the full the grace of Baptism in the total gift of self to the Love of the Father, in order to live like Christ, in the fire of the Holy Spirit, his same love for all the others."[27]

■ ■ ■

Sometime in the early-morning hours of January 8, 2011, after going to sleep at her husband's side, Stephanie Suzanne Teresa Wimmer Nooney passed away quietly at home, age forty-two. I took the train to New Jersey for her funeral and realized with sadness that it was the only time both our bodies were ever inside the same church.

Catholic funeral masses always remind me of Matthew 28:6: "He is not here; for he has risen." They place you right on the fault line between the "now" and "not yet" of redemption. You walk past the casket of your dead loved one, knowing that it contains only her body; she is not here. Then the priest gives you the Eucharist, and you realize your loved one is alive, united with you in the Body of Christ—closer to you than she had ever been in life. She lives.

CHAPTER 5
The Love That Liberates

Overcoming obstacles to forgiveness—with Blessed Laura Vicuña and St. Maria Goretti

[In] her dream she felt a sort of fire burning in her hand that did not pain her—it was the shining jewel she was bringing to her father. . . . She arose; her decision was made—the dream must become a reality.

—Hans Christian Andersen
"The Stone of the Wise Man"

A Catholic friend recently asked me to pray for a Muslim woman in one of the Persian Gulf states who is considering becoming Catholic but fears being ostracized. He told me that, when she was a child, the woman had a dream in which Mohammed reprimanded her severely for all the ways she had failed to be a good Muslim. Having been taught that dreams of Mohammed are always real, the frightened girl resolved to observe Islamic law perfectly—and did, to the best of her ability.

The years went by and the girl became a woman, still striving to be faultless in the practice of her faith. She hoped that one day Mohammed would once again appear to her in a dream, to let her know he was no longer displeased with her. But he never did. Instead, not too long ago, the woman dreamed of Jesus—who spoke to her quite differently than had Mohammed, my friend said.

Now, as a Catholic, I am thankfully not required to believe that private revelations are "always real"—otherwise I would have saved the prayer card a strange woman gave me depicting "Our Lady of Bayside, Queens." Just the same, the message the Muslim woman received in her dream of Christ struck me to the core.

Jesus said to her, "We only keep the good stories."

This is the voice of a loving father speaking to his child. I hear in it the promise in the Book of Revelation that God himself will dwell with human beings: "He will wipe away every tear from their eyes, and death shall be no more, neither shall there be mourning nor crying nor pain any more" (Rev 21:4).

■ ■ ■

When I was a child, reading the Passover story, I remember being surprised to read God's words to the Jewish people that the month including Passover "is to be for you the first month, the first month of your year" (Ex 12:2). It didn't seem to make sense, because Passover and the Jewish New Year's Day, Rosh Hashanah, occurred several months apart. Yet, I did get the feeling it meant there was something *new* about the Jews' exodus from Egypt, just as it was said at the Passover Seder that my family observed each year: "This night [is] different from all other nights." It was to be an absolute beginning.

Years later, on the third evening of Passover in 2006, I would experience an absolute beginning of my own. It was Easter Vigil, the night I received the Sacrament of Confirmation. In my mind, I am back there now. The light of the

Paschal Candle shines from the pulpit; a share of its flame flickers on the candle I hold as I listen to the chanting of the Exsultet (Easter Proclamation).

The Exsultet is a communal purification of memory—a "This Is Your Life" for the People of God. It recalls the most painful and damaging events of humanity's past, revealing their true meaning within the context of divine providence. The effect is like that of a camera panning back from an extreme close-up, revealing that what first appears to be a blotch of murky darkness is actually the center of a stunning sunflower. In the light of Christ—represented by the Paschal Candle—the Jewish people's dark period of slavery in Egypt is revealed as a necessary chapter in the world's most beautiful story. God's liberation of the Jews presages his ultimate liberation, freeing all humanity from sin and death. Past pain becomes prologue to future joy:

> These, then are the feasts of Passover,
> in which is slain the Lamb, the one true Lamb,
> whose Blood anoints the doorposts of believers.
>
> This is the night,
> when once you led our forebears, Israel's children,
> from slavery in Egypt
> and made them pass dry-shod through the Red Sea.
>
> This is the night
> that with a pillar of fire
> banished the darkness of sin.
>
> This is the night
> that even now, throughout the world,
> sets Christian believers apart from worldly vices
> and from the gloom of sin,

    leading them to grace
    and joining them to his holy ones.

    This is the night,
    when Christ broke the prison-bars of death
    and rose victorious from the underworld.

Why is *this* night, Easter Vigil, different from all other nights? Because the Resurrection begins the restoration of all things in Christ (Rev 15:2).

As the Exsultet's joyful strains fade into memory, the priest blesses the baptismal font. I see the vertical line of the Paschal Candle, representing the supernatural life of the risen Christ, intersect the horizontal line of the water's surface, representing the natural life of humanity. The symbolic union moves me to reflect upon how my own baptism, six years prior, built upon the life that began with my natural birth. It marked the start of my active participation in God's providential plan for me.

Thanks to my baptism, my life is no longer limited to a horizontal dimension, measured by how close or far I am on the journey toward death. It always has a *vertical* dimension, measured by how close or far I am on the journey toward heaven—a heaven that can be tasted on earth via the life of grace. These dimensions are my personal latitude and longitude, my spiritual global-positioning system; together, they form a cross.

In the Paschal Candle's glow, I see more deeply how God's loving presence has always been with me, like the pillar of fire that led the Israelites out of the darkness of slavery. And I begin to ponder how God permitted evil to enter my life only so he might draw from it a greater good. A verse of the Exsultet returns to mind: "O happy fault,

O necessary sin of Adam, which gained for us so great a Redeemer!"[1] Jesus can truly say, "We only keep the good stories," because all the good stories end in him.

■ ■ ■

During the months following my Confirmation, and especially as I began the habit of regular confession, I became increasingly conscious of the need to open more of the dark corners of my heart to Christ's healing light. In particular, I began to discover the extent to which the resentment I felt over my childhood abuse intruded upon my spiritual life. It was a time when, at the age of thirty-seven, I was first coming to terms with the enormity of what had been done to me as a child. What most disturbed me was the realization that, even after the abuse stopped, my relationship with my mother had remained unhealthily codependent. It was during this period that I attempted to discuss the abuse with my mother and was not satisfied with her response (see Introduction). I realized that for my own well-being, I needed to cut off contact for a time until I was capable of interacting with her without the fear of becoming absorbed. (I have since resumed contact with a better understanding of proper boundaries and reasonable expectations for my adult relationship with her.)

From my perspective, separating from my mother was an act of self-protection. But what was it from God's perspective? Might I be breaking the Fourth Commandment—failing to honor my father and my mother? This question became a real dilemma for me. I knew I had to seek the grace to forgive my mother: the Lord's Prayer commands us to forgive those who trespass against us. But did the Fourth Commandment require I stay in close touch with her even when such contact was, I felt, psychologically harmful to me?

Over time, with the help of friends, spiritual directors, and spiritual reading, I learned the tools of discernment for answering such questions. What is needed is an understanding of what forgiveness is and what it isn't.

Forgiveness is not the same as reconciliation. Forgiveness is interior, taking place in the heart of the one who forgives. Reconciliation, the ultimate goal toward which forgiveness tends, is a two-way street. Entrusted with the "ministry of reconciliation" (2 Cor 5:18), we are called to reconcile with those willing to be reconciled with us. However, if the offender is unrepentant, God requires only that we forgive him or her interiorly. I believe that is why Jesus, who bestowed forgiveness directly upon repentant sinners (such as the "woman of the city" in Luke 7:48), forgave his murderers only *indirectly.* Instead of saying, "Your sins are forgiven," he said, "Father, forgive them" (Lk 23:34). When the one who abused us continues to behave abusively, this intercessory prayer of Jesus—an outward expression of his interior forgiveness—becomes our model for fulfilling his commandment to forgive.

Forgiveness means letting go of resentment. We have seen that God permits evil only so that he may bring about a greater good (*CCC* 412). The greatest good possible is that we grow in grace. When we hold onto resentment toward the person who hurt us, we impede grace. Instead of being like Jesus' disciples, who gave up everything to follow him heavenward, we become like the rich young man of Matthew 19. He could have been another St. John, "the disciple Jesus loved," for Jesus looked upon him and "loved him." Instead, the young man "went away sorrowing" because he was unable to let go of the things that tied him to the earth.

Forgiveness does not mean forgoing the demands of justice. It means wanting God's best for that person. Where there is a crime, God's best can mean, in the words of Mark Shea, "releasing the evildoer into the hands of God's mercy even as you finger him to the cops."[2] St. Maria Goretti, as she lay dying, both forgave her attacker and answered the police's questions so he could be prosecuted. Both actions sprang from the same desire for her attacker's good and the good of others.[3]

God's best also means not letting the offender continue to offend. This bears upon discernment of how to observe the Fourth Commandment: If a parent is abusive, we fulfill the commandment by only having such contact with him or her as is safe.

Forgiveness means praying for the offender. This falls under the commandment to love your enemies and pray for those who persecute you (Mt 5:44). When the mere thought of an abuser stirs up painful memories, it can be a particularly difficult commandment to follow. A Sister of Life gave me some helpful advice: Ask Mary to place the offender within her Immaculate Heart; then, pray often for Mary's intentions. Prayer is vital to forgiveness because it connects you with the "circulatory system" of the Mystical Body of Christ—the graces that flow from its Head to its members.[4] The more you pray for your abuser, the more healing you will receive. This leads to the most important point:

Forgiveness is not within our own power. It is in *God's* power. Alexander Pope had it right: to err is human; to forgive, divine. In the Mass, when the bread and wine become, through transubstantiation, the Body and Blood of Jesus Christ, it is not by the priest's own power, but by the power of Christ acting through him. So too, when we pray for those who have offended us, we transform the detritus of evil into a seedbed of goodness—not by our own power, but by the power of the Holy Spirit working in and through us. The *Catechism* says that the effect of praying for our offender is so spiritually potent that it *purifies our memory*: "It is not in our power not to feel or to forget an offense; but the heart that offers itself to the Holy Spirit turns injury into compassion and purifies the memory in transforming the hurt into intercession" (*CCC* 2842, 2843).

All this is not to say that forgiveness is without pain. Union with Christ demands interior martyrdom (2 Cor 4:11). But we're in good company. The *Catechism* says our acts of forgiveness connect us with all the saints who gave their lives for the faith: "Forgiveness . . . bears witness that, in our world, love is stronger than sin. The martyrs of yesterday and today bear this witness to Jesus" (*CCC* 2844).

■ ■ ■

In the twentieth century, the Church recognized the sanctity of two young girls who were particularly profound witnesses to Christ's forgiveness: St. Maria Goretti and Blessed Laura Vicuña. The life stories of these "martyrs of chastity" speak deeply to victims of childhood sexual abuse, offering inspiration, guidance, and hope for healing. Yet, many Catholics do not understand why the Church honors them, as their legacy has been misrepresented both from within and without the Church.

Maria Goretti in particular has suffered from bad press. On one side, critics of the Catholic faith, particularly those opposing its sexual ethic, assert that her canonization proves the Church values a woman's physical intactness more than it values her life. On the other, some upholding her as a model of purity unwittingly reinforce the critics' view by implying she is called a martyr of chastity because she was not violated. The truth is that the term "martyr of chastity" does not refer to whether the saint died physically intact, but, rather, whether the saint died defending his or her purity. This teaching goes back at least to the time of St. Augustine, who wrote that Christian virgins who were raped before being martyred were still virgins (see Introduction).

The more I learn about Maria and Laura, the more I want to shout to their detractors and supporters alike: *These holy ones are not caricatures. They do not exist to satisfy an agenda. They are real young women.* It is worth taking the time to unearth their shining witness from beneath the politics and pious myths.

Born on October 16, 1890, in Corinaldo, a small town in central Italy, Maria was the third child of farm worker Luigi Goretti and his wife Assunta. Maria never learned to read or write, as her family was too poor to spare her for school. What the Gorettis did have in abundance was love and faith. Assunta in particular had a deep devotion to the Virgin Mary, and the family often prayed the rosary together.

Although influenced by her parents' faith, Maria had a devotional style that was all her own. She was naturally prayerful, maintaining a constant awareness of the presence of God. Pope Pius XII said in his decree of beatification,

> The Holy Spirit desired to enrich [Maria] . . .
> with special graces and extraordinary privileges
> increasing her sanctity every day: by means of
> natural and visible things, he drew her gently
> and sweetly to invisible and heavenly joys.
> . . . [Rejoicing] amid the gentle breezes and the
> brilliant sunshine, she raised her heart to the
> beauties of the heavens and with rapture even
> above the heavens to the choirs of angels, and
> then to the throne of the most High God, pour-
> ing out the joy of her heart even unto eternity.[5]

Although his language may seem syrupy, Pius seeks to capture a certain kind of longing that is essential to the life of faith. It is the same longing we saw earlier in St. Josephine Bakhita, who recalled her earliest stirrings of devotion as a pagan child in Africa: "Seeing the sun, the moon and the stars, I said to myself: Who could be the Master of these beautiful things? And I felt a great desire to see him, to know him and to pay him homage."[6]

This longing is something more than wonder, although wonder plays a part. It is the realization that God reveals himself to us on more than a merely spiritual level. Our relationship with him permeates our entire being, body and soul. In observing that God used "natural and visible things" to draw the young saint to "invisible and heavenly joys," Pius is telling us that Maria Goretti intuitively understood the true purpose of the body: to give glory to God. Like Thérèse of Lisieux, she refused to dissociate flesh from spirit. Instead, she sought to be fully integrated, so that the holiness of her soul might overflow into her body.

When Maria was eight, her father, seeking to save his family from desperate poverty, accepted an offer to work as a tenant farmer outside the coastal town of Nettuno. Because he lacked the funds to do it on his own, he entered into the tenancy jointly with a widower named Giovanni Serenelli. The Gorettis lived on one side of the upper floor of a barn, while Serenelli and his fifteen-year-old son Alessandro lived on the other; both families shared a central kitchen and stairs. It was an uneasy arrangement, as the Serenellis had a very different lifestyle from the devout Gorettis. Giovanni drank and brought home lurid magazines; Alessandro, a moody sociopath, used pornographic pictures from the magazines to decorate his room.

In late April of 1900, Luigi fell ill with malaria. The disease took several days to complete its fatal course. As he lay dying, fearing what might happen to his wife and children if they continued to live with the Serenellis, Luigi urged Assunta to move the family back to Corinaldo. He was forty-one when he passed on, leaving his wife with five children and a sixth on the way.

Giovanni lost no time in taking advantage of the mourners' vulnerability, demanding the family repay the debts he claimed Luigi owed him, and even propositioning Assunta. Horrified, the widow shunned his advance, but could not bring herself to follow her husband's dying wish. She had no wherewithal to make the move, and Giovanni insisted she and her family could not leave until their debts were paid.

Nine-year-old Maria, although devastated by the loss of her father, stayed strong for her mother's sake. She told her mother not to worry: she herself would take over household duties so Assunta could work in the fields. I see in her selfless action the experience of many children who are put in the position of having to protect an abused parent.

The fact that Maria now had neither father nor mother at home to protect her did not go unnoticed by Alessandro, now eighteen. Aware that she was concerned to preserve her purity, he set about confronting her with dirty jokes and stories while she was doing household chores.

How she responded to Alessandro's abuse brings us to one of the ways popular piety has unwittingly obscured the real Maria Goretti. Although the holy-card image of her as a gentle maiden bearing white lilies is symbolically accurate, it fails to capture her fieriness. She embodied the saying of G. K. Chesterton that the whiteness of purity should not be imagined as something antiseptic, like hospital walls: rather, "it means something flaming, like Joan of Arc."[7] And so, when she could not escape his sex talk, she hit Alessandro with whatever was at hand—a broom, an overturned bucket of water, anything to make him stop the flood of filth.

During the year following her father's death, Maria began to long to receive Holy Communion. She pressed her mother to let her have First Communion at age eleven, a year earlier than most children received it at the time. After some initial resistance, Assunta relented, and Maria was set to receive the Eucharist on May 29, 1902, the Feast of Corpus Christi.

Besides taking catechism classes, Maria brought a remarkable personal element into her preparation for reception of the sacrament: she approached each member of her family, as well as the Serenellis, to ask pardon for any offenses she might have committed. That might be typical behavior for a modern-day adult making the Eighth Step of Alcoholics Anonymous, but it has never been typical behavior for a child preparing for First Communion. It reveals how deeply she understood that being united with Christ's Eucharistic Body meant being at the same time united with his Mystical Body (Jn 14:20).

On the eve of her First Communion, Pope Leo XIII issued an encyclical on the Holy Eucharist that happens to both encapsulate the nature of Maria's holiness and presage her martyrdom. "[At] the present day," he wrote, "an insatiable appetite rages [for bodily pleasures,] infecting all classes as with an infectious disease, even from tender years."[8] He could have been describing Alessandro Serenelli. "Yet," the pope went on, "even for so terrible an evil there is a remedy close at hand in the divine Eucharist." He gave two reasons for this. The first was spiritual—"it puts a check on lust by increasing charity"—but the second touched on the mystery of the Incarnation: "The most chaste flesh of Jesus keeps down the rebellion of our flesh." We do not merely eat the Eucharist; we *become* the Eucharist. "St. Augustine makes Christ Himself say: 'You shall not change Me into yourself as you do the food of your body, but you shall be changed into Me.'"[9]

Maria felt changed on that Corpus Christi. After Mass, the priest asked the first communicants what they had requested of Jesus when they received him. When Maria's turn came up, she answered simply that she had asked him to let her receive him again. Like St. Ignatius Loyola in his *Suscipe* prayer, she could ask for nothing more.

At home, however, things were changing for the worse. That June, Alessandro twice grabbed her and attempted to force himself upon her. The first time, she was able to twist herself free, but the second time she had to dig her nails into his face to make him let go. Shaking his fist, he called out that if she breathed a word to her mother about the assault, he would kill her.

From then on, Maria begged her mother not to leave her alone in the house, but did not say why. Assunta, however, overwhelmed with working to meet Giovanni's demands for money, failed to recognize that her daughter was in danger. It was easy for Alessandro to arrange the circumstances where he could get Maria alone and make his final ultimatum.

■ ■ ■

There is no need to review all the details of Alessandro's brutal July 5 attack or the agony Maria endured before she died the following day. To understand why Maria is a saint, we need only look at two things she said during the last twenty-four hours of her life—the first, when she was attacked; the second, when she lay dying.

"No! No! I will not! It is a sin. God forbids it. You will go to hell, Alessandro. You will go to hell if you do it!" Those were Maria's words as Alessandro held up a knife and ordered her to submit—but just as noteworthy is what she didn't say. She didn't say *she* would go to hell; she knew it was no sin to be raped. Her concern was for Alessandro's soul. He was a member of the Mystical Body as much as she was. The love she bore for Christ prevented her from letting one of his members sin.

So why then, knowing the sin was not hers, did Maria continue to resist?

Step back with me for a moment. As a victim of sexual abuse, I live with the knowledge that, at the moments my abusers molested me, I was not a human being to them. I was an object. In a real sense, each abuser murdered me in his mind before he trespassed upon my body.

It was the same for Maria. She knew that Alessandro, in permitting himself to become sexually obsessed with her, had mentally depersonalized her. He refused to see that she was a child in need of his protection. All he could see was an instrument for his own gratification.

When Christians were being persecuted in ancient Rome, there were some who fled town rather than staying where they might be martyred. Their flight did not make them sinners—but neither did it make them heroes. They simply chose not to bear witness with their blood against the evil of persecution. In the same way, had Maria not put her entire strength into resisting Alessandro, she would not have sinned—but neither would she have been heroic. Instead, she *was* heroic, because she chose with her blood to bear witness against the dehumanizing evil of lust.[10] That is why the Church honors her as a "martyr of chastity."

We are not all called to blood martyrdom. But we are all called to holiness, and Maria shows us the way to it with her entire life—not only with her death.

"For the love of Jesus, I pardon him, and I want him to be with me in heaven." That was Maria's response when her parish priest, before giving her what she knew would be her final Communion (known as viaticum, when the Eucharist is given as "food for the journey" to heaven), asked if she could imitate Jesus' forgiveness of the penitent thief and forgive Alessandro.

Maria's forgiveness reveals that she embodied chastity on a eucharistic level. Recall Leo XIII's explanation of the two ways the Eucharist heals disordered desires. Both are present in Maria's answer: the "love of Jesus" and the will to incorporate the Savior's chaste love into her own actions. Chastity finds its highest expression in mercy: forgiving from a wounded heart makes the body most like that of the risen Christ. Those who evaluated her cause for beatification found it no coincidence that Maria's heart poured out its pardon on the day the Church marks as the Feast of the Most Precious Blood.

During the beatification process, it became known that Maria's act of forgiveness had a sequel. Alessandro, released from prison after serving twenty-seven years for the murder, told Vatican investigators that he had initially been unrepentant—until the night, eight years into his sentence, when Maria appeared to him in a dream. She carried fourteen white lilies, which she handed to him, one by one. Each flower, as he took it, became a white flame, like a candle. Alessandro realized with emotion that the flowers represented her forgiveness for every one of the fourteen stab wounds he had inflicted upon her.

A few years after his release, Alessandro sought and received Assunta's forgiveness. He went on to become a tertiary (lay associate) at a Capuchin monastery, living in prayer and penitence, and tending the monastery's flowers.

■ ■ ■

Born in Santiago, Chile, in April 1891, Laura Vicuña was the first child of army officer Joseph Vicuña and his wife, Mercedes Pino. Shortly thereafter, political persecution forced her family to flee to a remote village.

Joseph died of pneumonia when Laura was two, just after he and his wife had a second daughter, Julia. The widowed Mercedes opened a dressmaking business, which she ran until one day in 1899, when thieves broke in and took all her stock. Left in dire poverty, she decided to take her daughters to Argentina in hope of a better life.

The family settled near Junin de los Andes, where Mercedes met Manuel Mora, a *ranchero* known for his cruelty. Desperate to get back on her feet, the mother agreed to be Mora's *mujer* (live-in woman), moving with her daughters into his home on his main ranch.

It soon became clear to Mercedes that she was not the only object of Mora's lust: he also desired Laura, then only eight years old. The mother bid to protect Laura and Julia by enrolling them in the College of Mary Help of Christians, a local boarding school run by the Salesian Sisters.

Laura thrived in her new environment—so different from the Mora ranch, where she and her family had lived in fear of the master's violent rages. Life at Mary Help of Christians was ruled by St. John Bosco's motto, "To serve the Lord with joy." With the Blessed Sacrament close at hand in the chapel, Laura developed a strong devotional life, drawing spiritual strength from the Real Presence. She told her spiritual director, Fr. Augusto Crestanello, "It seems to me that it is God himself who keeps alive in me the awareness of his divine presence. Wherever I am, in class or in the playground, this knowledge is with me and it helps and strengthens me."[11]

The priest was concerned. Would not such constant meditation distract her from her responsibilities? "Ah no, Father," Laura replied. "I know that this thought helps me do everything better and does not disturb me at all, because it is not that I am always thinking of it but that without thinking of it directly at all, the memory makes me happy."

Laura's answer reflects her remarkable spiritual maturity. She instinctively understood the role memory plays in shaping the believer's identity in Christ.

We can understand what Laura was describing if we think of how our motor memory works. That is the part of our memory that enables us to do a sequence of physical actions without having to constantly intellectualize each one. For example, if you are learning to ballroom dance, at first you have to juggle numerous things in your mind, counting the beats while connecting each one with a different motion. But, given time and practice, you can internalize the correct movements to the point where you no longer need to consciously keep track of them (unless you have two left feet like me). Your body remembers what to do so that your mind is free to enjoy the presence of your partner.

In the same way, we could say that once Laura, through her visits to the Blessed Sacrament in the tabernacle, learned the steps to practicing the presence of God, she internalized the memory of those steps. From then on, no matter what she was doing, she could be mindful of the movements of the Holy Spirit, responding without missing a beat.

One day at school, one of the Salesian Sisters addressed the girls about the importance of the sacrament of marriage. As the sister spoke, Laura experienced deep spiritual anguish as the reality of her family situation hit her with full force: her mother was living in sin. From then on, she turned her full energies toward praying that her mother would free herself from Mora.

As she grew in the life of faith, Laura told Fr. Crestanello that "the presence of Jesus in the Eucharist led her to
feel the presence of Mary."[12] Like so many abuse victims
who have found comfort in Our Lady's arms, she realized she needed a mom in heaven to help her better love
her mom on earth. She would later say, as she lay dying,
"My greatest comfort is my devotion to Mary. . . . She is
my mother!"

Laura felt the need for Mary's maternal protection
most strongly during school vacations, when Mora pur-
sued her relentlessly. Local villagers whispered that the
rancher was sending the girl to school because it was she,
and not her mother, whom he intended to marry. One
night at a fiesta, when she refused the drunken ranchero's
invitation to dance with him, he threw her out into the
dark Andean wilderness. He then ordered Mercedes to go
out and persuade her daughter to come around.

The image of the mother urging her ten-year-old
daughter to placate a pedophile is heartbreaking, showing how much Mercedes was in thrall to her abusive lover.
When she returned to the fiesta having failed in her mission, the furious Mora tied her to a post and whipped her.

Mora's reaction to Laura's defiance was to cut off
funds for her schooling. The Salesian Sisters took pity on
her, waiving her tuition and letting her remain in resi-
dence during vacations. Thanks to their aid, she was able
to avoid returning home for nearly two years.

In the spring of 1902, shortly after receiving the Sacrament of Confirmation, Laura begged Fr. Crestanello's
permission to make an extraordinary sacrifice. She wanted
to offer her life to God for her mother's conversion. After

some consideration the priest gave her his consent, believing the desire to be inspired by the Holy Spirit.

It would not be long before Laura's desire was fulfilled. She fell ill in July 1903, and over the next two months it became apparent that she had pulmonary tuberculosis. Her mother took her home, where Mora immediately resumed his attempts to abuse her.

Seeing how Laura's strength waned as she fought Mora's advances, Mercedes began, for the first time in years, to show some strength of her own. She rented a small house in the village near the school so she could look after Laura and Julia in safety.

Mother and daughters enjoyed peace until the night of January 14, 1904, when Mora, drunk, crashed their dwelling and insisted on staying the night. Laura, although terribly weak, tried to make a run for the school. She had just managed to get out the door when Mora caught her and began to whip her in the street.

Laura's cries brought neighbors outside. Unnerved by the crowd, Mora put the ill girl across his horse, but then had second thoughts. Tossing her onto the street, he rode away.

What little health Laura had left deteriorated quickly. Fr. Crestanello was called. After he heard her confession and gave her absolution, he asked her a few questions. In the presence of others, she told him she forgave Mora and bore him no ill will. Only she and the priest knew that her apostolate of forgiveness was not over. The supreme act had yet to come.

On the afternoon of January 22, a Salesian missionary gave viaticum to Laura as her mother and two classmates stood by. The dying girl indicated she wished to speak privately with her mother, so the others gave them some distance. It was then that Laura revealed she had offered her life for her mother's conversion. This revelation succeeded in reaching Mercedes where all the girl's pleadings over the past several years had failed. Mother and daughter embraced.

Laura called over the priest. "Father, my mother has promised to leave that man." A great peace had spread over her face. A few moments later, she passed away uttering prayers of thankfulness to Jesus and Mary.[13]

■ ■ ■

At the Easter Vigil Mass, before the Paschal Candle is lit, the priest embeds five grains of incense into the candle in the form of a cross, symbolizing the wounds of Christ. As he sinks the grains into the wax, he says, "By his holy and glorious wounds, may Christ our Lord guard us and keep us." Only after these wounds are called to memory does the light of the Resurrected Christ, symbolized by the ignited candle, shine forth and spread its glow to every candle in the church. If all the stories in Christ are good, bathed in the light flowing from his wounds, what does that say about the stories that remain in me now that I, through my Baptism, live in his light?

CHAPTER 6

The Love That Grows Deeper

Drawing closer to God and to one another—with Dorothy Day

> In these northern regions, a beech-wood often
> buds in a single night and appears in the morn-
> ing sunlight in its full glory of youthful green.
> So, in a single instant, can the consciousness of
> the sin that has been committed in thoughts,
> words, and actions of our past life, be unfolded
> to us. When once the conscience is awakened,
> it springs up in the heart spontaneously, and
> God awakens the conscience when we least
> expect it.
>
> — Hans Christian Andersen
> "Anne Lisbeth"

For six years during my twenties, while suffering from the suicidal depression I now know was due to post-traumatic stress disorder, I sought help from a well-known psychiatrist in New York City.

Some people are surprised when I tell them the Ivy League–trained doctor, who had excellent professional credentials in the area of suicide prevention, failed to diagnose my PTSD. The reason is simple: like many in the psychiatry profession, he was trained to see sexual activity as an unqualified positive. As a result, he did not see any connection between my desire to commit self-harm and my putting forth a sexually provocative persona. It never seemed to occur to him that perhaps I was a victim of sexual abuse who was trying to hide my vulnerability by projecting a false self. Quite the contrary, in fact: the behavior a more enlightened therapist would have seen as a pathology, he saw as a sign of health. He believed it his role to help rid me of whatever remaining hang-ups were preventing me from leading a fully "liberated" lifestyle.

Our sessions were like the sacrament of confession in reverse. I would recount the various things I had done to try to distract myself from my depression. Usually they involved thinking about, or engaging in, acts I now know as sins against the Sixth and Ninth Commandments, such as sexually objectifying others and encouraging them to view me as a sex object. After forty-eight minutes, the psychiatrist, after expressing his approval of how "self-actualized" I was becoming, would recite his favorite maxim, "We will be called to account for joys not taken."

The words of my psychiatrist's saying were from the Talmud (the Jewish oral law), but he was taking them completely out of context. He was confusing mere pleasure with joy. Pleasure is rooted entirely in sensation. Dogs can have pleasure. Joy is rooted in the mind and heart. It is a divine gift that can be experienced only by persons. Because it is not tied to sensory experiences, we can experience joy even in the midst of suffering. If the doctor had conveyed the true meaning of the maxim, it would have helped me understand what was missing from my life. Instead, he simply tossed it out as if to say, "Go and sin some more."

Eventually, after years of such therapy, seeing that my despair continued to worsen, I finally had the wisdom to switch psychiatrists. However, it was not until I received the grace of faith in Christ that my self-destructive thoughts abated. Over time, that same grace led me to discover the extent to which my building up a hyper-sexualized front had failed to protect me from the effects of abuse, as I described in chapter 3. Aided by prayer, scripture, and—after entering the Catholic Church—the sacraments, I let go of my false self. Instead, I learned to live with the fact of my vulnerability by behaving with respect for my own dignity and that of others.

The Sacrament of Penance aided me enormously in learning how to live out my authentic identity in Christ—but first I had to learn that confession is not the same as therapy. First, there is the obvious difference that one is a sacrament and the other isn't. No matter how much a psychiatrist may charge, sharing in Christ's power to forgive sins will always be above his pay grade. But, beyond that, there is another fundamental distinction: therapy is all about me, while confession is all about me as seen in relation to God. This second distinction is hard to describe on paper, but, as I would discover, it becomes clear in practice.

I have to smile when I recall my early confessions. They can be summed up in three words: too much information. Today I know that, although there are times when giving context can be helpful, my duty is fulfilled when I reel off my sins, note how frequently I committed each one, and sincerely repent. Back then, however, I was under the mistaken notion that no confession was complete without copious backstory. Priests tried to tell me they didn't need to hear all the details, but old habits died hard. A bit of divine providence was necessary to set me straight.

It was Advent 2006; I had been Catholic for eight months. After spending the afternoon volunteering on Manhattan's Upper East Side, I entered a confessional inside the Church of St. Vincent Ferrer, where I found a grandfatherly Dominican. At that time, my first book *The Thrill of the Chaste* had just come out. I was completely taken up with the excitement of being a first-time author, to the point where everything else in life, including my relationship with God, was taking a distant second place. There was no question that I had material for confession. But how to begin?

If it were today, I would say something like, "I've been preoccupied with feelings of pride; I've repeatedly failed to refer glory back to God; I had feelings of envy a few times," and so on. Instead, I began, "You see, Father, I wrote a book—"

The priest's eyes brightened and he suddenly seemed years younger. "Really?" he interrupted. "*I* wrote a book!"

"Oh, uh, really?" I said. "That's great!" And the priest chatted happily about his literary work—still in print after twenty years, available on the leading retail website, yada yada yada—while I listened politely, thinking, "But I want to talk about *my* book, not *your* book." Thankfully, after a minute, we both remembered where we were, and I completed my confession—with slightly more humility than when I entered the room.

But only slightly. For, not long after New Year's Day, I was back in the confessional, this time at the Church of St. Francis of Assisi in midtown Manhattan, near the offices of the *Daily News* where I was working at the time.

This time, my confessor was an aged Franciscan. Having learned nothing from my previous experience, I again said, "I wrote this book, and . . ."

"Really?" A delighted smile spread across the old priest's face. "*I* wrote a book!"

It finally hit me that perhaps God was trying to tell me something.

■ ■ ■

Dorothy Day (1897–1980), an adult convert to the Catholic faith, knew what it was like to want to confess about a book. Today, the cofounder of the Catholic Worker movement, whose cause has been introduced for canonization, is often called an "American Mother Teresa" for her work helping the poor and suffering. In 1924, however, she was a long way away from the peace she would find laboring in God's vineyard. That year, she published the novel *The Eleventh Virgin*, about a woman who, in a desperate attempt to keep her boyfriend, submits to an abortion. It was in fact Dorothy's own story—an attempt under the guise of fiction to process her lingering pain and grief over the abortion she had undergone five years before.

After entering the Church in December 1927, Dorothy grew increasingly ashamed that details of her past sins remained in the pages of *The Eleventh Virgin* for all to see. Describing this period of her life to a friend decades later, she recalled that the more she thought about the novel, the more convinced she became that she had "to track down every copy of [it] and destroy them all, one by one"—even if it took her the rest of her life. "I'm as ashamed of *that* as anything: the sin of pride if ever there was an example of it." The fear that people might find the book in libraries kept her awake at night. "I even tried to find out how many libraries there are in the country."[1]

Finally, Dorothy revealed her obsession to a priest in a confessional. His first reaction was laughter. Relieved, Dorothy thought he would simply advise her to get her priorities straight. She was in for a surprise:

> I will remember to my last day here on God's earth what that priest said: "You can't have much faith in God if you're taking the life he has given you and using it that way." I didn't say a word in reply. He added, "God is the one who forgives us, if we ask him; and it sounds like you don't even want forgiveness—just to get rid of the books."[2]

Then the priest quoted St. Paul: "You are our epistle, written in our hearts, which is known and read by all men: Being manifested, that you are the epistle of Christ, ministered by us, and written: not with ink but with the Spirit of the living God: not in tables of stone but in the fleshly tables of the heart" (2 Cor).

The scripture's wisdom touched Dorothy's soul. She was expending her energy trying to destroy what she had written on dead trees, when she should have been showing the world what God had written on her heart—a living love letter meant to be "known and read by all."

> Since then, [Dorothy admitted,] I still think about that book of mine. I still hope that no one who hasn't read it ever will. But I'm not as worried as I used to be, and with each year I forget [about it] more and more. But you can't forget your life, and even if God has forgiven you, . . . what was wrong was wrong, and we

have our memories for a reason—to learn from
our mistakes and not keep repeating them.[3]

■ ■ ■

Dorothy's experience illustrates a truth I came to discover for myself: While confession is not therapy, it *is* sur-
gery. For me, as a cancer survivor, I think of it as having a
malignant tumor taken out.

Knowing I have something inside me that may be
deadly, I present myself to the "surgeon"—that is, the
confessor. I identify for him, as best I can, what the evil
thing is that must be removed. Since he is trained to diagnose ailments of the soul, it is possible he may tell me that
some of the things I think are malignant are not at all serious. However, if these mild ailments are tangled up with
a malignancy, a confessor who is a good spiritual director
will help me discern where the non-sinful thoughts cross
over into sinful ones.[4] Such a confessor is like the expert
surgeon who was able to remove my cancerous thyroid
without damaging the vocal cords that surrounded it.

At the same time, through the sanctifying grace
bestowed in his absolution, my confessor—or, rather, the
Divine Physician acting through him—initiates an effect in
the spiritual realm far beyond anything my surgeon could
accomplish in the physical realm. Another cancer analogy
is helpful here. Even with my thyroid removed, and even
in the wake of my post-operative treatments, there will
always be some leftover thyroid cells in my system. These
cells are not necessarily cancerous, but past experience
indicates they are particularly prone to cancer. Likewise,
no matter how sincerely or how often I confess, there will

always remain in me the *fomes peccati*—Latin for "tinder for sin," better known as concupiscence.

To understand concupiscence, it helps to understand what was lost by original sin. Adam and Eve, before their disobedience, were each perfectly ordered from the top down. Body was subject to soul, passions were subject to reason, and reason was subject to God. Since they were so perfectly integrated, it was impossible for sensations arising in their bodies to move them to seek their own will over that of their loving Creator.

Then came the first sin, sending the perfectly ordered human edifice into a state of disarray. Body rebelled against soul, passions rebelled against reason, and reason rebelled against God. Through the graces of Baptism, and the renewal of baptismal graces through the other sacraments of the Church, the human person is reconciled with God, but the inclination to sin remains. Concupiscence, the umbrella term for that inclination, includes the temptations to lust, pride, envy, gluttony—all the things society tries to excuse as "looking out for Number One."

Returning to the cancer analogy, if even a single thyroid cell remains in my body, no possible good can come of it—only the potential for a new malignancy. And that is precisely where the analogy breaks down. So long as I resist falling back into sin, the sanctifying grace of the Sacrament of Penance turns my potentially malignant inclinations into instruments that work toward my perfection. Fr. John C. Edwards, S.J., calls this effect of the sacrament the "consecration of weakness." It enables Christ to enter into our life in a new way, much as he does in the Anointing of the Sick. When a cancer patient receives the Anointing,

Fr. Edwards writes, even if it does not result in a physical healing, "still Christ did touch that cancer":

> The effect is that cell by cell as it grows, moment by moment, in every event of the sickness— painful, depressing, humiliating—it is confer- ring the life of Christ. The invalid has a sort of built-in mechanism of sanctification; the very thing that is weakening him, will put him into his death agony, put him into eternity, is, in fact, making him holy as it happens. The answer to all his needs is in the very disease. . . .
>
> [In] the Sacrament of Penance, . . . it is not a physical cancer which is touched, but a spiri- tual one. The root sinfulness, deeper perhaps than words can express, has been put before Christ and his Church; and Christ touches. That root of sin [the inclination to sin] may not be cured, but it is now a weakness consecrated to Christ. It will continue, but touched by Christ it is now a continual appeal not just for mercy, but for union: the man is holier because of his sinfulness.[5]

A traditional blessing confessors may give after absolv- ing a penitent encapsulates this "consecration of weak- ness." Invoking Jesus' Passion, the merits of the Blessed Virgin Mary, and of all the saints, the priest prays, "May . . . whatever good you do and whatever suffering you endure heal your sins, help you grow in holiness, and reward you with eternal life."[6] With this blessing, the Church tells me that God does not merely heal my wounds. When I unite my heart to the Sacred Heart of his Son, whose own wounds are now glorified, he heals me *through* my wounds. Through God's great love and mercy, my own sufferings become occasions of grace, salvation, and—most mysteriously—joy.

Another perspective on the healing power of the sacraments comes from Sarah Dickerson, a wife and mother who gives marriage-preparation talks for the Archdiocese of Philadelphia. When Sarah was eight years old, a female friend showed her a stash of hardcore pornography (belonging to the friend's father). The brutally exploitative images profoundly unsettled young Sarah. "From then on," she says, "I frequently obsessed about sexual things."[7] At the same time, her home situation was tense, as her mother and father were "terribly mismatched." "Sexual obsession and preoccupation became my escape from my parents' dysfunctional marriage." Formed by this preoccupation, she went on to make "a host of destructive decisions" as a teenager and young adult. "I yearned for and sought out healing while continually tripping up in sexual sin."

During her freshman year of college, Sarah's search for healing led her into the Catholic Church. She saw the Church's teachings on sin and reconciliation as providing a means of overcoming the pessimism instilled in her by the evangelical Protestantism in which she was raised:

> For instance, I was taught that we are *utterly depraved* as a result of original sin, while the Catholic Church teaches that we are *profoundly wounded* by original sin. The Catholic understanding of our profound woundedness has truly been essential to my continued healing, for it allows room for the divine fingerprint beneath the mess within each of us.
>
> "And God saw that it was good," Genesis tells us of creation, including man and woman

[see Genesis 1:26, 31]. At our fundamental core is goodness. . . . [The] grace of the sacraments active within us is ever uncovering that goodness, seeking to restore us to innocence, and to deliver us from our wounded sexuality. Don't underestimate the power of the sacraments, the power of God's very life in us, to help us make better, different, more life-giving choices.[8]

■ ■ ■

I know from my own experience that sacramental grace really does work to heal the damaged will. At the same time, while many Catholics—not least of all converts like Sarah and myself—witness the sacraments' transformational power, their enthusiasm can be misleading. Grace is not magic. It may motivate us in the short run to make positive decisions, but if it is to have a lasting effect, it requires our ongoing cooperation. What's more, even given our best efforts, healing ultimately happens in God's time, not ours. If we want to see a shining example of how cooperation with grace can, over time, lead a deeply wounded person to fulfillment in Christ, we need look no further than Dorothy Day.

In her autobiography, *The Long Loneliness*, Dorothy makes a general observation that women are concerned with the things that are necessary for family life—home, children, and "especially love."[9] "And in their constant searching after it," she adds, "they go against their best interests."[10] It is her way of explaining why, before her conversion, she behaved in ways that were ultimately damaging to her. She was trying to fill a hole in her heart—a hole deepened by the wound of parental rejection.

Growing up in a Chicago apartment, Dorothy—the third of five children—greatly admired her father, sportswriter John Day, despite his being emotionally distant, controlling, and so absorbed in work that he neglected his family. Dorothy's mother, Grace, seems to have dealt with her husband's self-absorption by burying herself in homemaking duties. Although Dorothy felt great tenderness toward her, Grace comes off in *The Long Loneliness* as more dutiful than doting.

Dorothy is very forgiving of her father's behavior. She admits he treated her "like a child," keeping tight reins on her until she graduated high school at sixteen. Jealous for his privacy, he prevented her and his other children from having friends over, while at the same time barring them from going out to visit friends. "It seems to me we had much time to ourselves, much time alone," she admits. I am disconcerted by the way she tries to explain away the neglect, seeming to sense she has complained too much: "The fact that father kept us from going out, and did not want company to come in, saved us from the busy existence that most persons had."[11]

Her desire to be truthful finally gets the better of her when she tells of the "sad summer afternoons when there was nothing to do":

> Our parents did nothing to offer us distraction
> and entertainment. We were forced to meet our
> moods and overcome them. There were times
> when my sister and I turned to housework from
> sheer boredom.[12]

It was at this time that faith began supplying the ten-year-old Dorothy with a level of joy far beyond anything she had experienced at home. Although the Days were not religious, a local Episcopal pastor convinced Grace to let her sons sing in his church's choir. Dorothy began attending church and became overwhelmed by the beauty of the hymns. The abundant gratitude of the *Te Deum* and *Benedicite* opened up a world of wonder that would, in her young adulthood, become for her a principle of return—bringing her back from the precipice of morbidity and despair. [13] She was baptized and confirmed in the Episcopal Church.

More cause for gratitude emerged when Dorothy was fourteen and received the blessing of a new brother, John, who would be the last of the Day children. She fell in love with the baby, caring for him as though he were her own. Witnessing his discovery of the world's sights and sounds renewed her own delight in God's creation.

Even the most simple acts of hugging and kissing the baby brought her deep joy, for he was the only member of the family with whom she was permitted to be physically affectionate. Her parents never hugged their children; the only physical affection she received from her mother was a "firm, austere kiss" every night. (The way she describes it, I think of the kind of peck that says, "Okay, I kissed you, now go away.") "We were like most Anglo-Saxons," Dorothy explains, which is perhaps true, but it does not seem to have made her adolescence any easier. [14]

Complicating things further was her growing interest in the opposite sex. With all displays of affection being off-limits, including the most innocent contact with family and friends, learning how to become a fully integrated woman was a real challenge. She sensed a connection between the physical things that delighted her senses and the spiritual things that delighted her soul, and was frustrated at the seemingly unbridgeable divide between the two. Years later, she would observe, "The disassociation of the flesh from the spirit is evil and a bitter fruit in the mouth."[15]

Dorothy entered the University of Illinois on an academic scholarship in the fall of 1914. At first, coming from such a restrictive home environment she was thrilled at her newfound freedom, but the novelty soon wore off. Within a few months, she was overcome with feelings of desolation, crying morning and night. When she tells of this sadness in her autobiography, she attributes it to "homesickness," but her words make clear that its source was not any real longing for home. It was her inability to bear being separated from John, then two years old.

In her parents' failure to meet their children's emotional needs—especially their neglecting to demonstrate appropriate expressions of love—Dorothy's experience resonates with me as a sexual-abuse survivor. Considered in that light, it is not surprising that when her emotional pain became too much for her, she adopted a false self.

She was then beginning to develop a strong sense of solidarity with the suffering masses, brought on by reading the social-justice authors of her time and seeing the urban slums that sparked their concern. The anger she felt at the plight of the poor added to her bitterness at being away from the brother who had been her main source of affection. Sensing her emotional vulnerability, she resolved to survive by rejecting all that symbolized softness—beginning with faith.

Karl Marx's line about religion being an opiate of the people gave Dorothy the excuse she sought to create a rebellious persona that would be the antithesis of her former piety. She began taking the Lord's name in vain to mark herself off from the Christians she knew, whose presence reminded her of the weakness she sought to shed. "Because I was unhappy at being torn from my child, my baby brother, I had to turn away from home and faith and all the gentle things in life and seek the hard."[16]

Yet she could not harden her heart to the needs of those less fortunate. "Our Lord said, 'Blessed are the meek,' but I could not be meek at the thought of injustice. I wanted a Lord who would scourge the moneylenders out of the temple, and I wanted to help all those who raised their hand against oppression."[17] Radicalism gave her the outlet she needed to take her mind off the vacuum in her heart. The masses became her great love. She joined the Socialist Party and began developing her writing talents in hope of using them to change the social order.

In June 1916, the Day family moved to New York City after Dorothy's father found work at a newspaper there. That was too much distance for Dorothy, then eighteen. She quit school to move back in with her family and, she hoped, become a newspaper journalist.

When Dorothy describes returning to live at home, the theme of parental rejection immediately returns. Her father sabotaged her search for a job, instructing his editor friends to tell her, if she came knocking, that a newspaper was no place for a woman. When, after months of searching, she finally got hired at poverty wages by a Socialist paper, her father's response, with her mother's full support, was to cast her out onto the street. "[No] daughter of his was going to work and live at home."[18] Dorothy's exile had begun—and, with it, her "constant searching" for the love she lacked.[19]

That searching led her into the depths of the radical subculture. At the time, she believed herself to have only the highest motives for surrounding herself with loose-living revolutionaries: she sought to win freedom for the poor, the oppressed, and the downtrodden. Later, looking back after her conversion, she saw that other factors had been at work—"my own self-love, my own gropings for the love of others, my own desires for freedom and for pleasure."[20]

As she writes those words in *The Long Loneliness*, Dorothy intentionally avoids mentioning the most damaging result of her efforts to fulfill her desires: the abortion she had in 1919 when she was twenty-one. The man by whom she was pregnant, Lionel Moise, was, like her father, a newspaperman. He was glad to have her as a live-in lover, but had no interest in commitment. One writer observes— accurately, I think—that "[the] abusive Moise was likely a stand-in for Day's emotionally distant father, and the abortion was Day's attempt to hold on to him at any cost."[21] It didn't work; before she had even recovered from the procedure, Moise walked out on her.

The loss of boyfriend and child left Dorothy utterly bereft. One day not long after her abortion, in the apartment she and Moise had shared, she turned on her gas oven without lighting it and put in her head to ingest the fumes. A neighbor smelled the gas and ran inside, saving her life.

Dorothy continued to live emotionally unanchored until 1925, when she and a man she had come to love deeply began living together. Forster Batterham, an anarchist who worked as a biologist, shared both her passion for radical causes and her desire for domesticity. They moved into a small house in a laid-back beach community on Staten Island, and Dorothy enjoyed a kind of peace she had not known before.

Yet it was, she realized, a restless peace. All she had wanted since she left home was now hers: a stable relationship with a man she loved, a beautiful place to live, a circle of friends, and a burgeoning writing career. Just one thing was missing: someone to thank.

The gratitude that had welled up within her as a child was back with overpowering force; she had to let it out somehow. The only answer, she realized, was to "[begin] consciously to pray more."[22] Her prayer grew in ways she had not known when she was a practicing Episcopalian. She found comfort in saying the rosary and attending Sunday Mass. The Catholic Church appealed to her in its authenticity and universality. For all its pomp and splendor, it remained the church of the people. "My very experience as a radical, my whole make-up, led me to want to associate myself with others, with the masses, in loving and praising God."[23]

Such newfound joy was not without cost. As her prayerful attitude showed forth in daily life, she was anguished to discover that, like the Garden of Eden in reverse, following God's call would cost her the greatest earthly paradise she had known.

■ ■ ■

In the light of her growing faith, Dorothy began to notice the differences between herself and the atheistic Batterham that she had previously chosen to overlook. Whereas her radicalism stemmed from a love of people, his stemmed from a bitter distrust of humanity. Dorothy admired the natural beauty surrounding their home, and saw in it the same divine generosity that created men and women. The man she loved admired the same nature and resented human beings for failing to display such perfection.

Batterham particularly reviled the institution of marriage, ranting against the "tyranny of love."[24] "It was hard for me to see at such times why we were together," Dorothy admits, "since he lived with me as though he were living alone and he never allowed me to forget that this was a comradeship rather than a marriage."[25]

While she continued trying to win over a man who, like her father, placed his love out of reach, Dorothy felt her heavenly Father pursue her. In June 1925, she learned with joy that she was pregnant again. Batterham, like Moise before him, protested against becoming a father. This time, however, Dorothy refused to let her fear of abandonment prevent her from attaining her dream of motherhood.

That she was pregnant at all was a wonder, for, after her abortion, she had thought she was unable to have children. Yet, even as she felt God was saving her from being "unfruitful," she feared that his seeming generosity might prove to be a cruel joke.[26] She later wrote to a friend, "I always rather expected an ugly grotesque thing which only I could love; expecting perhaps to see my sins in the child."[27] When the baby, born in March 1926, proved to be a beautiful little girl, Dorothy saw her as a living sign of divine mercy.

Naming her daughter Tamar, Dorothy began to take instruction in the Catholic faith so the baby could be baptized in the Church. "I felt that 'belonging' to a Church would bring that order into her life which I felt my own had lacked."[28] Batterham objected vehemently, but Dorothy again found the strength to overrule him. On the day of Tamar's baptism in June 1926, realizing it was a matter of time before Dorothy too would enter the Church, he punished mother and child by storming out of the celebratory party.

Behind Dorothy's desire to have Tamar know "belonging" was the sense that, even in her closest intimacy with Batterham, she herself lacked that belonging. Union with the Church was, she realized, the only way out of her "long loneliness"—"a spiritual hunger . . . that was in me, no matter how happy I was and how fulfilled in my personal life."[29]

Despite his initial opposition to fatherhood, Batterham quickly grew to love Tamar. The bond Dorothy felt with him in sharing parental duties, along with her desire that the baby grow up with two parents, led her to delay entering the Church. She hoped against hope that, with prayer and the passage of time, Batterham might agree to marry her. "It was killing me to think of leaving him."[30]

The couple's tensions continued for some months until an argument led Batterham to again walk out. When he returned, two days after Christmas 1927, Dorothy refused to let him into the house. The following day, leaving Tamar in the care of her sister, she was baptized conditionally at a Catholic church (in case her Episcopalian baptism was invalid) and made her first confession. She would receive her first Holy Communion the next morning. After a lifetime of seeking, she was finally in the arms of "a kind Father who is so far above our earthly fathers that he will forgive us all our sins, even the greatest, who will not give us a stone when we ask for bread."[31]

In *The Long Loneliness,* Dorothy does not say how it
felt to hear for the first time *"ego te absolvo"*—"I absolve
you"—and know the forgiveness of God. Her later attempt
to destroy the remaining copies of her novel suggests that,
although she intellectually believed in the Sacrament of
Reconciliation, she had yet to accept the full reality of
divine mercy. Still, I would like to think that given her
desire to make reparation for her abortion, she saw yet
another sign of God's mercy in the providential timing
of her reception into the Church. It was the day when the
Church honors those martyred when Herod, in his jeal-
ousy over reports of the birth of the Messiah, ordered his
soldiers to kill all the boys in Bethlehem and its vicinity
who were age two or younger (Mt 2:16). On that Feast
of the Holy Innocents, Dorothy Day—who so regretted
ending an innocent life—made her own life an acceptable
sacrifice to the Lord.

■ ■ ■

The loss of Batterham left Dorothy hungering for com-
panionship. Over the next five years, she strove to fill the
empty space—mothering Tamar, going to daily Mass and
weekly confession, and continuing to write—but the longing remained. Then God worked a change in her, the kind
of change I believe he works in every wounded person
who desires it and is patient with the workings of grace.
He transformed her heart so that, instead of seeking to
gain love, she sought the grace to give love, to love God
through loving her fellow human beings: "I offered up a
special prayer, a prayer which came with tears and with
anguish, that some way would open up for me to use what
talents I possessed for my fellow workers, for the poor."[32]

The following day—December 9, 1932—she met Peter Maurin, the idealistic French expatriate who gave her the vision for the *Catholic Worker* newspaper and apostolate. Maurin sought to bring Mystical Body theology—the teaching that we are all one in Christ—into every area of human work, study, and fulfillment. It was a tall order, to be sure, but Dorothy presented it in the pages of the *Catholic Worker* in terms that helped readers incorporate it into their daily lives. By the time she died in 1980, her impassioned call for Catholics to live the Gospel values of peace, prayer, penance, and mercy had reached millions of people around the world.

Perhaps the greatest insight Dorothy added to Maurin's vision was her recognition of the prayers of the Church, especially the Mass, as the foundation of all Catholic activity in the world. She taught that ideals of universal brotherhood find their proof and fulfillment in the holy sacrifice where Christ is really present on the altar. Jesus pours himself out for us, so that we might, in union with him, pour ourselves out for others. "I would not dare write or speak or try to follow the vocation God has given me to work for the poor and for peace, if I did not have this constant reassurance of the Mass, the confidence the Mass gives. (The very word confidence means 'with faith.')"[33]

After leaving Batterham, Dorothy remained unmarried and chaste for the rest of her life. It was not always easy, especially early on. But as the *Catholic Worker* grew, she came to realize that she was not truly alone, nor was Tamar her only child. "I am a mother, and the mother of a very large family at that. Being a mother is fulfillment, it is surrender to others, it is Love and therefore it is suffering. He hath made 'a barren woman to dwell in a house, a joyful mother of children' [Ps 113:9]."[34]

She became an instrument of healing for many wounded souls. More than thirty years after her death, the memory of her maternal love remained fresh in the mind of Catholic Worker volunteer Mary Lathrop:

> [Dorothy was] a spiritual mother, but also really the ideal substitute because my mother and I had a very distant relationship. My mother and stepfather were highly critical. I knew that no matter what I did, I would not be good enough. But Dorothy really accepted me completely as the person I was. She didn't tell me I wasn't good enough, she did not tell me I should be other than I was; it was just total acceptance, which was new for me.[35]

Lathrop's experience reflects how Dorothy practiced what she preached. Believing Christ to be "present with us today in the Blessed Sacrament just as truly as when he walked with his apostles," she brought the love she received in the Mass into her everyday interactions.[36] "When Dorothy was present," says Catholic Worker colleague Jim Forest, "she was completely present."[37]

Reading stories like these, I admire how, with God's grace, Dorothy was able to give others the compassion she herself lacked as a child. So it is with surprise that I read Lathrop's next words about her experience of Dorothy's spiritual motherhood: "It wasn't a huggy-kissy kind of relationship. The affection was spiritual, but sometimes when I was visiting with her, and before I would say goodbye, she would want me to come and give her a little light kiss before I left."[38]

"A little light kiss." Lathrop's words recall Dorothy's description of her own mother's "firm, austere" goodnight kiss. After reading in *The Long Loneliness* about how her parents' withholding physical affection led her to experience a disturbing "conflict" between spirit and flesh, my initial reaction is disappointment.[39] I want to believe she overcame all the effects of her childhood wounds. I want to think she grew out of her youthful sense of dissociation. I want to see that she did not turn into her mother.

Then I reread Lathrop's words about receiving "total acceptance," and I am ashamed of my self-centered idea of what a saint should be. Dorothy, in giving herself completely to God through neighbor and to neighbor through God, embodied a spiritual motherhood that was truly beyond anything she herself had received. What's more, she never claimed to have perfectly reconciled flesh and spirit. On the contrary, this great woman, who began her autobiography with a story about going to confession, bore her childhood wound with the humility of one who has consecrated her weakness. She is never quite at home in the body (but, then, neither was St. Paul—see 2 Corinthians 5:8), yet her unease is always mixed with godly wonder. "A woman contemplates her body, 'that earthen vessel,' that temple of the Holy Spirit, and young or old it is always holy."[40]

Like St. Thérèse of Lisieux, whose Little Way inspired her Catholic Worker philosophy, Dorothy's path to holiness was one of continuous conversion.[41] She modeled the merciful love that Blessed John Paul II, in his encyclical on divine mercy, said "marks out the most profound element of the pilgrimage of every man and woman":

Authentic knowledge of the God of mercy, the God of tender love, is a constant and inexhaustible source of conversion, not only as a momentary interior act but also as a permanent attitude, as a state of mind. Those who come to know God in this way, who "see" him in this way, can live only in a state of being continually converted to him. . . . [It] is this state of conversion which marks out the most profound element of the pilgrimage of every man and woman on earth.[42]

How beautifully fitting that these words of John Paul II happened to be published the day after the completion of the earthly journey of Dorothy Day—whose *Catholic Worker* column was called "On Pilgrimage."

CHAPTER 7

The Love That Radiates

Living out your call to holiness— with Blessed Margaret of Castello and St. Bernard of Clairvaux

> Can you realize the happiness of that moment of assurance when the soul understands its mission? That moment, when the sorest wounds from the thorny path, even if caused by one's own fault, are healed and forgotten in spiritual health and strength and freedom. . . . Then the thorny path shines like a path of glory around the earth.
>
> —Hans Christian Andersen
> "Thorny Road of Honor"

If you could ask Jesus one question, what would it be? The story is told that St. Bernard of Clairvaux, who is ranked among the Doctors of the Church, had that opportunity when Christ appeared to him in a vision. Bernard asked him if during his Passion he received any wounds that were unrecorded by the Gospel writers. In other words, he sought to know if Jesus had any *hidden* wounds.

It is not the sort of question that many people would think of asking the Lord. I suspect the usual questions Jesus receives begin with "why." Such questions often (though not always) contain an implicit complaint, like that of Job (Jb 13:24)—"Why dost thou hide thy face, and count me as thy enemy?" Bernard's question, however, treats the Lord not as an adversary, but as an intimate friend. Perhaps that is why his question, unlike Job's, received an answer.

In answering Bernard, Jesus did more than reveal a previously unrecorded wound. He said his hidden wound was the most painful of all those he received. It was the wound on his shoulder as he bore the burden of his Cross.

■ ■ ■

As best as I can discover, the story of Bernard's vision falls under the category of "pious legends"—those stories of saints which, while perhaps not literally true, give authentic insight into the nature of their particular holiness. Bernard himself bore deep, hidden wounds, dating from his youth. In his adult life as a Cistercian monk, his greatest comfort came through recognizing how his vulnerability brought with it the opportunity to draw closer to Christ.

Born in 1090 into a noble household near Dijon, Burgundy, Bernard was a man of strong passions and great love. In the history of saints and especially monastics, he qualifies as one of the greatest "people persons," deeply devoted to his family, friends, and religious brothers.

Bernard's youth was different from many of his wealthy peers, in that at a time when childcare duties were typically assigned to servants, he benefited from a mother who was very present for all her children. An early account of his life notes that she insisted on nursing her children herself, rather than engaging a wet nurse as would be expected.[1] The same account adds that she also fed her children spiritually, teaching them the Catholic faith. The care she gave to Bernard's body and soul seems to have prepared his mind for a major theme of his theology: It is the love of God, entering into our human flesh, that enables us to truly love one another.

When Bernard was seventeen, the death of his mother threw him into an emotional tailspin. Although he had spent the past several years at a boarding school, her love had remained his anchor, while her high expectations had strengthened him against temptation. Without her in the background, the handsome and charismatic teenager, who could so readily become attached to people, felt vulnerable and exposed. Being given to strong passions, the danger of falling into sexual sin became very present for him.

More than one woman sensed his vulnerability and tried to take advantage of it. Once, he and some friends traveling together were offered hospitality by a married woman. The hostess gave Bernard a bedroom separate from his friends, under the pretense of showing the noble youth special honor. Then, during the night, she entered his chamber. Seeing her, he shouted, "Thief! Thief!"

Confused, the woman ran out, lit a candle, and joined the rest of the home's residents to search for the thief. When none was found, everyone went to bed again. After a time, the woman again entered Bernard's chamber, only to get the same response. She even tried a third time, hoping to break the saint's will, but to no avail. Finally she gave up and went to bed.

The next morning, continuing on their journey, Bernard's friends chided him for waking them up three times over a "thief" who existed only in his nightmares. He answered them, "There really was a thief, because my hostess tried to take from me a treasure that cannot be replaced."[2]

Don't let Bernard's choice of words put you off: he knew (or at any rate would eventually know when he studied theology) that no one could "steal" his chastity, since there is no sin without consent. What he was trying to convey was a feeling common to abuse victims—that of being personally invaded by a predator who wants what he or she has no right to have. His words also express with admirable candour the hurt he felt upon being subjected to a manipulator whose very hospitality was a lie. The hostess's actions were those of an abuser: isolating him from those who could have protected him, coming to him at a time when she knew he would be at his weakest, and hoping to benefit from the uneven power relationship. She knew that, as a well brought-up gentleman, he would not fight a woman, nor would he dare insult her on her own turf, where she could easily frame the situation as though she were the abused party.

After that incident and another like it, Bernard chose the religious life, entering the recently established community at Citeaux in 1112. He felt the duty to pursue the highest level of holiness, and feared that if he delayed deciding, his worldly loves—including attachments not only to people but also to literature—would take the place of God in his life. As divine providence would have it, those same loves put at God's service would not only bring Bernard to sanctity, but—thanks to his writings—would also inspire countless others to live holy lives. The masterly literary quality of his preaching, combined with his great sensitivity to human pains and longings, would lead

future generations to call him the Mellifluous Doctor—
meaning his words flowed like honey.

■ ■ ■

Bernard did not enter Citeaux alone. His popularity
was so great that some thirty other men joined the abbey
with him, including two of his five brothers. Two more of
his brothers entered soon after; eventually his youngest
brother and even his father would follow.

Although his relationships with friends and family
would be shaped by his new brotherhood with them in
religious life, Bernard's affections were never purely spiri-
tualized. Whether loving Christ or neighbor, he always
loved as a human being, rejoicing in the human qualities
of his beloved. A sermon he gave after nearly twenty-five
years in religious life reveals his deep understanding of
our natural need for a love that is embodied:

> Notice that the love of the heart is, in a certain
> sense, carnal, because our hearts are attracted
> most toward the humanity of Christ and the
> things he did or commanded while in the flesh.
> The heart that is filled with this love is quickly
> touched by every word on this subject. Noth-
> ing else is as pleasant to listen to, or is read
> with as much interest, nothing is as frequently
> in remembrance or as sweet in reflection. . . .
>
> I think this is the principal reason why the
> invisible God willed to be seen in the flesh and
> to converse with men as a man. He wanted
> to recapture the affections of carnal men who
> were unable to love in any other way, by first
> drawing them to the salutary love of his own

humanity, and then gradually to raise them to
a spiritual love.[3]

The saint's words remind me of how our hyper-sexualized culture damages us by encouraging us to think of love in superficial terms—reducing emotional love to the physical, and physical love to the sexual. In fact, the opposite is true: emotional love *transcends* the physical, while physical love *transcends* the sexual.

I say this not to deny the fact that the love we feel draws upon our physical experiences of our loved ones but, rather, to affirm it. My own love for friends and family is by nature embodied, wrapped up with the way I receive their physical presence. I remember how, for example, from earliest childhood I associated my father with the smell of Old Spice.

At the age of nine, four years after my parents' divorce, I was grieved when my father moved with his second wife to a city thousands of miles away. For years after, the fragrance of Old Spice would unleash a flood of emotions. It evoked the subliminal sense that my father was physically present, followed immediately by the pained realization that he was *not* present. The feeling of having hopes raised and then instantly dashed made me cry.

Today I see my father often, as we are again living in the same city, and he still wears Old Spice, though he doesn't splash it on as heavily as he used to. (Back in the seventies, men *really* overdid colognes.) The fragrance makes me happy in the comfort of continuity: it reminds me that the father who loved me when I was a child is the same father who loves me today. It also makes me thankful that I still have a chance to make up for the times I failed to show him love in the past.

Perhaps it is that same continuity that makes my heart swell when I take in the odor of incense at the high Mass on Sunday. Frankincense is, after all, the base note of Old Spice. It is as though God knew that associating the scent with my earthly father's presence would point me to his own fatherly love, poured out through the Real Presence of his Son. There too, at the Mass, I am given a chance to make up for the times I have failed to love my heavenly Father.

■ ■ ■

In 1115, Bernard became the founding abbot of the Cistercian abbey of Clairvaux, an office he would hold until his death thirty-eight years later. Although he always retained his capacity for personal friendship, he felt the need to restrain his sensitive nature to provide the stability expected of a spiritual father. One memorable morning in 1138, however, while attempting to preach a sermon on the Song of Songs, he gave his spiritual sons an unexpected glimpse into his personal cross of suffering.

At the time of that sermon, Bernard, having just buried his older brother Gerard (who had long been with him at Clairvaux) could no longer hold back his emotions. Nearly nine hundred years later, the abbot's tears still seem to jump off the page as he speaks with gut-wrenching honesty about his hidden wound of grief—one made all the more painful by his efforts to keep up a brave face:

> How long shall I keep my pretense while a
> hidden fire burns my sad heart, consumes me
> from within? . . . For when he was taken away,
> . . . my heart departed from me too. But up till
> now I have done violence to myself and kept

up a pretense, lest my affection should seem
stronger than my faith.[4]

Bernard admitted that, while he performed the grave-
side funeral rite "with dry eyes," his calmness was a front:

> Since then, all the time, I have forced myself to
> refrain from much weeping. . . . But the sorrow
> that I suppressed struck deeper roots within,
> growing all the more bitter, I realized, because it
> found no outlet. I confess, I am beaten. All that I
> endure within must needs issue forth. But let it
> be poured out before the eyes of my sons, who,
> knowing my misfortune, will look with kind-
> ness on my mourning and afford more sweet
> sympathy.
>
> You, my sons, know how deep my sorrow
> is, how galling the wound it leaves. . . .[5]

Recalling the personal sacrifices Gerard made to fulfill
his duties managing the abbey's domestic life, Bernard
says "[he] shouldered every burden that I might be free
. . . to enjoy the delights of divine love, to preach with
greater facility, to pray without anxiety." He adds, "I was
saluted as abbot, but he was the one who watched over
all with solicitude." Now he is overcome by the "manifold
anxieties" from which his brother had protected him.[6]

Reading Bernard's anguished lament, I am reminded
of the pious legend of his conversation with Jesus, and
wonder if its origins lie in this very sermon. Bernard
reveals a deep gash of grief in his soul—one all the more
painful because, with the departure of the brother who
had shared his cross, the "burden" of the abbey now falls
entirely on his shoulders: "In my loneliness I groan under

the burden. Because your shoulders are no longer there to support it, I must lay it down or be crushed."[7]

As in the legend, Bernard wants to know if heaven has any sympathy for his hidden wound. Thinking out loud, he wonders if perhaps Gerard is so consumed with the joy of the beatific vision that he no longer cares what happens to the brother left behind on earth. Then suddenly, he answers his own question: "But God is love, and the deeper one's union with God, the more full one is of love."[8] Here is where, with a striking epiphany, Bernard breaks forth into the glorious words of hope that Pope Benedict XVI has quoted many times: *Impassibilis est Deus, sed non incompassibilis*—"God cannot suffer, but he can *suffer with*."[9]

"Therefore," Bernard goes on, again addressing Gerard,

> you too must of necessity be merciful, clasped as you are to him who is Mercy; and though you no longer feel the need of mercy, though you no longer suffer, you can still be compassionate. Your love has not been diminished but only changed; when you were clothed with God you did not divest yourself of concern for us, for God is certainly concerned about us. All that smacks of weakness you have cast away, but not what pertains to love. And since love never comes to an end, you will not forget me forever.[10]

I believe that, in recognizing that the brother who compassionately suffered with him on earth now through union with Christ continues his compassion in heaven, Bernard finds the true location of Jesus' hidden wound. It is in *us*. Our hidden wounds—all our mourning, all our traumas, all our leftover disorders that snag us like briars as we strive to grow in grace—all these, Christ has made his own. We have been crucified with Christ; it is no longer we who live, but Christ who lives in us (Gal 2:20).

What is more, we know that the saints are with Christ: as it is with him, so it is with them. The saints too cannot suffer, but they can *suffer with*. That is how I discovered the Communion of Saints—through a saint's compassion for my own wounded soul.

■ ■ ■

At the time in 1999 when I received the gift of faith (see chapter 3), I knew I wanted to enter a church—but had no intention of entering *the* Church.

The person to whom I looked as my model for Christian living was my mother, who herself had undergone a dramatic conversion almost fifteen years earlier. Her faith had led her to become Catholic, but she quickly grew dissatisfied, opting to continue her Christian journey outside the Church. I recall that she told me the Church adhered to rituals and traditions that she considered "unbiblical," including devotion to the saints.[11]

I accepted Mom's opinion of the Catholic faith unquestioningly because she had supposedly "been there, done that." Moreover, not yet having come to terms with my childhood abuse and the emotional dependency it engendered, I was unaware of the extent to which I longed to please her.

So, being baptized on Pentecost 2000 at a local church—an Adventist congregation whose pastor indulged me when I asked for a "generic baptism" without specific Adventist baptismal promises—I set about trying to find a denomination to call home. In the meantime, I began the process of converting my life. Although I still loved music, my discomfort with the entertainment business—particularly its promotion of sexual objectification—made me want to move on from the world of rock journalism. Eventually, I found work on the copy desk of the *New York Post*. While not exactly the most sexually enlightened place (it copied the British tabloid practice of featuring photos of scantily clad women), it was a step closer to mainstream journalism. At the same time, seeking to allay the isolation I felt as an unchurched convert in the heart of New York City, I sought fellowship online—reading and commenting on Christian blogs, and sharing my own journey on my blog The Dawn Patrol (dawneden.blogspot.com). Although I remained proudly resistant to entering the Church, the topic that interested me the most as a writer was what Catholics called the "culture of life."

It was a time when the workings of grace were gradually showing through in my behavior. I was letting go of my false self—the sexually aggressive persona I had created to shield my vulnerability—and learning how to act with integrity. In that sense, although I remained ignorant of the effects of my childhood abuse, I began to stop acting out of my woundedness. In another sense, however, I continued to act as a wounded child—using my blog to lash out at people who reminded me of my abusers.

Under the guise of defending Christian teachings on marriage and the sanctity of life, I picked fights with radical feminist bloggers, calling them names and attacking them in personal terms. They offended me because I saw in their writings the attitudes that had enabled my abuse. In their denial of the personhood of the unborn child, I saw the denial of the personhood of all children. In their praise for what they termed sexual freedom, I saw the elimination of sexual boundaries—the boundaries that, had they been enforced in my childhood home, would have protected me from harm. In their ridicule of modesty advocates, I saw my mother's laughter at me when I, as a child, complained of her and her boyfriend's household nudity: "Oh, she's becoming *modest*." In their efforts to convince young women that purity was "repressive," I saw the culture that had enabled the efforts I made to "free" myself by means of sexual encounters that served only to re-traumatize me. In their advocacy for "sex workers," I saw the encouragement of the damaging lie that sex is "only physical." (To this day, I cannot understand how people can simultaneously decry the sexual objectification of women while insisting upon the "right" of women to sell their bodies.) Even though I was not yet able to name the pathology of dissociation (described in chapter 3), I knew that trying to separate body from soul was a deadly game.

While I don't want to be too hard on my younger self, it is clear to me now that in excoriating feminist bloggers, I was not fully conscious of the extent to which I was acting out of misplaced anger. As Christians, we are called not just to speak the truth, but to speak it in love (Eph 4:15). My good desire to make a public stand for truth was mixed with an unhealthy desire to punish people for sins committed against me by others.

This habit of acting out of my anger—an anger stemming from my wound of abuse—spilled out one day into my job performance. The consequences would change my life forever.

■ ■ ■

Working on the evening shift of the *Post* copy desk meant being the last pair of eyes to review stories before they went off to the printer. My duties were to write headlines, correct errors in spelling or grammar, and notify the editors of any obvious factual errors or omissions. One day in January 2005, I was given a news article to copyedit that had an obvious bias against the personhood of unborn human life. I had received such stories in the past and been disturbed at having to copyedit them. This time, something snapped and I could not take it anymore.

Because of the way the story was written, there was no way I could simply make it neutral. It would either be biased as it already was, in a manner denying the unborn's personhood by referring to a developing child as a thing rather than a human being, or biased in a manner affirming such personhood. For one brief moment, I thought of asking the city editor for permission to alter the bias in favor of life, but, knowing her, I was certain that permission would be denied. If that happened, then, believing as I believed, my only remaining choice would be to refuse the story—which would likely get me fired. In three years on the job, I had refused a story only once—it included a graphic description of a scene from a pornographic film. My editor was so angry that he told me that the next story I refused would cost me my job.

Dorothy Day writes, "Our desire for justice for ourselves and for others often complicates the issues. The supernatural approach when understood is to turn the other cheek, to give up what one has, willingly, gladly, with no spirit of martyrdom. . . ." The contrary approach is to follow the "devices and desires of my own heart."[12] I was so taken up with my own conception of "justice" that I was unwilling to follow Jesus all the way to the Cross. Instead, hoping I might have my own way with the story and yet keep my job, I decided to alter the story's bias surreptitiously—altering a few key words so that the offending angle was reversed.

When the story came out the next morning with my changes intact, the reporter who wrote it immediately demanded my firing. My supervisor, the copy chief, was stunned, because I had never made unauthorized changes before. He recommended I apologize to the reporter, which I did, but it wasn't enough to pacify her. Over the next few evenings, my supervisor valiantly tried to convince the editors to give me a second chance, while I sat at my desk and waited for the axe to fall.

Staring at my computer on one of those nights—for I wasn't being given many stories to copyedit—I felt like a failure. Not only had I failed my employer, but in breaking St. Paul's dictum to serve my employer as I would serve the Lord (Eph 6:5–8), I had failed God. At that moment, more than anything, I wished I had a friend in heaven.

As a good Protestant, I tried to tell myself, "Jesus is my friend in heaven." True enough! But I still could not get the idea out of my head that I needed *another* friend in heaven. However present Jesus' love was for me at that moment, from my perspective it felt distant and remote. I needed someone who had worked in the media, who had lived during a time like mine, who could reach out to me and help me find my way back to God. In other words, I needed a saint.

Until that time, I had been fearful of asking saints' intercession. Based on what my mother and other Protestants had told me, I believed it was idolatry. It seemed that praying for the intercession of a saint would only put an obstacle between God and myself. Besides, I thought, why would the saints care about me anyway? Weren't they just looking at God all the time? It never occurred to me that perhaps, even as they looked at God, the saints might also be looking at me, seeing me as I exist in the mind of God, and loving me.

Finally, feeling I had nothing to lose—wasn't I on the outs with God already?—I opened up my computer's Web browser and searched for the keywords "patron saint journalists." One of the names that came up—a twentieth-century Polish Franciscan friar named Maximilian Kolbe— was, according to the Patron Saints Index (saints.sqpn .com), a patron of not only journalists, but also the pro-life movement. *Great*, I thought. *I can just pray to him and kill two birds with one stone.* My thinking was that I would just pray to this one saint, once in my life, to satisfy this mysterious desire that was nagging at me. Then I would have done with it and never pray to a saint again.

Yes, I know. Heaven must have shaken *very* hard with laughter over that one.

Before asking St. Maximilian's intercession, I wanted to learn a bit about his life, so I searched a bit more and found a detailed biography on a Catholic website. It said that, beginning in the 1920s, he spearheaded an international media apostolate, publishing newspapers and magazines spreading devotion to Jesus through Mary.[13] That explained why he was a patron of journalists. As I read on, an unexpected bit of information made me burst into tears. It said that in December 1939, when Poland was occupied by Nazi Germany, Maximilian "began to organize a shelter for 3,000 Polish refugees, among whom were 2,000 Jews." He had risked his life to save people who might very well have been my relatives.

Wiping my tears and checking to make sure none of my coworkers had seen me cry, I read on to discover why Pope John Paul II had canonized Maximilian as a "martyr of charity." It was because of his manner of death—sacrificing his life to save the life of another. While imprisoned by the Nazis at the Auschwitz concentration camp in late July 1941, he witnessed an SS guard condemn ten prisoners to die in a starvation cell as punishment for the escape of a member of their cellblock. As one of the prisoners was about to be hauled off, he shouted in despair, "Oh, my poor wife, my poor children. I shall never see them again." Hearing the cry, Maximilian immediately stepped forth and offered his own life in the condemned man's place. Amazingly, the guard acceded to his wish.

More than forty years later, the man whose life Maximilian saved, Franciszek Gajowniczek, attended his canonization.

Reading of the saint's great love affected me beyond words. I looked around again; it was late, and no one in the newsroom was paying attention to me. Remembering the advice Catholic friends had given me in their unsuccessful attempts to get me to petition Mary, I swallowed my pride and began speaking to Maximilian as I would speak to a friend: "Dear St. Maximilian, I'm in trouble, I'm about to get fired, please pray for me . . ."

I think that is as far as I got. The next thing I remember is feeling overwhelmed by a great *whoosh!* It was as though grace rushed down from heaven—a comforting, embracing, protective grace, like being in the eye of a hurricane.

Suddenly, I knew with inexplicable certainty that even if I was fired, I was going to be all right, because asking St. Maximilian's prayers had realigned me with the will of God.

In that moment, the Church's teaching on the Communion of Saints was opened up to me. With amazement, I realized how wrong I had been about asking saints' prayers. How certain I had been that such petitions would distance me from God! Instead, they drew me *closer* to him, by drawing me closer to a holy person who was united to him.

■ ■ ■

I was indeed fired, and then, a few months later, hired by the *Post*'s main competitor, the *Daily News*. In between, I made the decision to enter into full communion with the Catholic Church. I knew the saints were with Christ, and if they were in the Church, then I had to be there too. Over time, I would come to believe the truth expressed by St. Joan of Arc during her trial: "About Jesus Christ and the Church, I simply know they're just one thing, and we shouldn't complicate the matter" (CCC 795).

Fascinated by St. Maximilian, I began to read as much about him as I could. That led me, inevitably, to Mary, because Maximilian never ceased to praise the woman he lovingly called "the Immaculata" (and sometimes simply "Mom"). For a time, I retained my Protestant reluctance to give honor to Our Lady, fearing that veneration of her might take my attention away from God. Yet I could not deny that Maximilian, whose entire spiritual life was founded upon devotion to her, was now in heaven.

Certainly, then, Marian devotion would not *prevent* my getting into heaven . . . and perhaps it might even help?

My hesitation to venerate Mary, like my hesitation to request a saint's intercession, seems funny now, but there were deeper psychological reasons why I resisted getting close to her: she frightened me. I was afraid of her purity.

My fear was really a fear of being judged, because Mary's purity made me conscious of my own impurity. In one sense, I had felt myself to be impure from childhood, because of being abused and being in an environment where my innocence was not respected. That feeling, I now realize—and I hope you realize, after reading this far—was completely erroneous. While it is sadly typical for child-hood sexual-abuse victims to blame themselves for what was done to them, such blame is completely misplaced. Being abused does not make you impure, as I discussed in the introduction. In another sense, however, I really was impure—not because of what had been done to me when I was helpless, but because of decisions I had made of my own free will as an adult. How, I wondered, could Mary possibly want to have anything to do with me?

To repeat the familiar saying of G. K. Chesterton, while society tries to paint chastity as a dull, antiseptic shade of white, it is really "something flaming like Joan of Arc."[14] That was the fire I saw in Mary, and I feared getting burned by it. But, under the guidance of St. Maximilian's writings, I got closer to the flame—beginning with acquiring a Miraculous Medal and praying the medal's prayer: "O Mary conceived without sin, pray for us who have recourse to thee."[15]

The Miraculous Medal features Our Lady of Grace as she looked in one of her apparitions in 1830 to St.

Catherine Labouré, a young French nun. Our Lady stood before Catherine with her arms outstretched, revealing many rings on each of her hands. The rings were bedecked with gemstones from which brilliant rays streamed forth. Our Lady said, "These rays symbolize the graces I shed upon those who ask for them. The gems from which rays do not fall are the graces for which souls forgot to ask."

When I first read those words, they haunted me. How many times, in my fear of getting close to Mary, had I failed to ask for graces? The medal reminds me to ask for them whenever I need them—which is to say, all the time.

Through Maximilian's writings, I learned that the Church calls Mary the Mediatrix of Grace because it believes that the Holy Spirit, having come upon her after she gave her "yes" at the Annunciation (Lk 1:38), never left her. Mary remains forever united with the Holy Spirit, and, as our heavenly Mother, longs to bestow that same Spirit upon us.[16]

Yes, Mary is aflame; the *Catechism of the Catholic Church* tells us she is the burning bush (Ex 3:2), radiating fire without being consumed (*CCC* 724). But hers is a *purifying* fire—purifying us so that she might draw us ever closer to herself, under the loving protection of her mantle. She does this always out of love, not out of a desire to judge us or humiliate us. You can see this love in Our Lady of Grace's hands. She does not hold them up like a traffic cop, to push us away. Her palms are always open, inviting us near. Through drawing us with maternal care into her own love, she enables us to grow in that same Holy Spirit love—the love that will draw us closer to one another and to God.

Society's great lie is to tell us that the Church's promotion of Mary's purity is founded on judgmentalism. There is indeed judgment, but it is our own sins that judge us. It is never Mary's purity. Her purity is what *saves* us from the judgment of sin, when we in love and repentance enter into her purifying embrace.

■ ■ ■

When Blessed Margaret of Castello (1287–1320) was born, her parents thought she was anything but pure. The wealthy couple, who lived in a castle on a mountain outside of Florence, Italy, were aghast to discover that their first child—whom they had so hoped would be a boy—was not only a girl, but a deformed one. Margaret was blind, dwarfish, and extremely hunchbacked. Her head was large in proportion to her body, and one of her legs was much shorter than the other, which would come to cause her great difficulty in walking. Because of her deformities, her parents resolved to hide her rather than have anyone know they had brought such an unattractive child into the world.

From an early age, Margaret showed intelligence, kindness, and great devotion to God. The priest chaplain at the castle taught her prayers, and by the time she was five, she was visiting the castle's chapel every day. She was very joyful and did not realize she was different from other children her age. The girl's exuberance, however, only served to aggravate her parents, as it made it more difficult for them to prevent visitors to their castle from discovering her existence. So they took it upon themselves to inform her that she was not like other children, but was in fact an ugly freak who should remain hidden.

When Margaret was six, she met a visitor in the chapel and mentioned innocently that she was the daughter of the castle's lord and lady. Upon learning of the incident, her parents, terrified that others would discover their secret, decided to send her away to live in a tiny cell built along-side the parish church. They pretended the move was for their daughter's own good. After all, she already enjoyed being in church, and, since she was sightless, there was less chance she would get hurt than if she were navigating the large castle.

It is not clear how the little girl's physical needs were met in her cell—probably there was a servant to bring her food—but it seems the only person who visited her regularly was the parish priest. He was saddened at her parents' insistence that she live away from prying eyes, but, given that they were powerful—her father was governor of the local military garrison—there was nothing he could do. Margaret, retaining her cheerfulness, told him she was thankful to be able to share in the sufferings of Christ. This attitude of joyful abandonment to divine providence would characterize her throughout her life.

Margaret remained in her isolated cell at the church until she was eighteen. Her parents then moved to another town and took her with them—but again hid her, this time in their castle's dungeon. A year later, hearing reports of miraculous cures issuing from the tomb of a priest, her parents finally dared to bring her out into the open. They brought her to the tomb in the city of Castello and told her to kneel down there among the throngs of pilgrims and pray for a cure. Meanwhile, they sat at a distance—no doubt hoping no one had noticed that they had walked in with the blind, hunchbacked girl—and watched to see what would happen. When, at the end of the day, Margaret was still kneeling with all her deformities still visible, her parents went home without telling her. They simply dumped her, leaving her in the tomb with the sick and the dead.

The next morning, when Margaret was unable to find her parents, some beggars took pity on her and helped her find the inn where they had stayed. There, she learned from the innkeeper that her parents had gone home without her—she was truly alone. It is said that, despite her sadness at being abandoned, she never spoke against her parents, but went on loving them and praying for them.

Margaret begged on the streets of Castello for a time, but her holiness was so evident that poor families in the town began to invite her to stay in their homes. After about a year, her reputation for sanctity reached a local convent of cloistered nuns, which invited her to enter. Margaret was happy to do so, being eager to live in a religious community whose Rule was one of silence and personal sacrifice. Once there, however, she discovered that the Rule was not observed—the nuns chatted freely and accepted expensive gifts from outsiders. When Margaret complained to the superior, she was told to do as the other sisters and ignore the Rule. She refused, and before long the order cast her out onto the street.

I have to pause in amazement. How cold these nuns must have been, to reject a blind and handicapped young woman because her desire to observe their own Rule caused them embarrassment. Those who have been abused by people claiming to be Christian clearly have a friend in Blessed Margaret.

For several months, as Margaret returned to begging, the townspeople ostracized her, believing she must have done something terrible to be rejected by the convent. However, her visible holiness again won out. A family took her in, and she was invited to enter the Mantellate, a Dominican lay religious order whose members lived in their family homes or in the homes of benefactors. As a daughter of St. Dominic, she spent the remainder of her life praying and doing works of charity, including caring for the sick and visiting prisoners. Her spiritual life continued to deepen, and she revealed to her confessor that at Mass, despite her blindness, she could see Christ upon the altar.

Margaret was thirty-three, the age of Christ crucified, when she died in 1320. After her funeral at the town church, the townspeople physically prevented the Dominican friars from carrying her to the Mantellate cemetery. Arguing that she was obviously a saint, they insisted she be buried right there at the church. The townspeople and the friars disputed as Margaret's body lay on a pall; meanwhile, a crippled girl was carried by her parents to the body and was immediately healed. That was enough evidence to sway any doubters. The Dominicans gave Margaret's body a mild form of embalming—enough to preserve it for a week—and she was interred at the order's church, which quickly attracted pilgrims.

More than two hundred years later, on June 9, 1558, as Rome began to consider her cause for sainthood, Margaret's body was exhumed. When her coffin was opened, her body was found to be incorrupt. Her kind, homely face; her hunched back; her unevenly matched legs and misshapen feet—all remained as they were on the day of her death. Her skin, hair, teeth, and nails were all intact—and, if you have the opportunity to visit her shrine at Città di Castello's Church of San Domenico, you will find that they still are.

God preserved Margaret's body as if to show the world that the little girl who was rejected by her parents is accepted and loved by her heavenly Father. Her hunched shoulders, still intact, remind us that she who, on earth, carried her share of the Cross now lives in heaven. There, united with us in the Body of Christ, she longs for us to ask her help bearing our crosses. All the saints, despite no longer having sorrow or tears or pain, do *"suffer with"* us in a mysterious way—and for them it is pure joy.

CHAPTER 8
The Love That Heals

Finding our past, present,
and future in the Eucharist—
with St. Thomas Aquinas and
Blessed Karolina Kózka

> The brightness is too great. We have not yet
> eyes that can look directly at all the glories God
> has created, but someday we shall have them,
> and that will be the most beautiful fairy tale of
> all, for we ourselves shall have a part in it.
>
> —Hans Christian Andersen
> "The Toad"

Fr. Michail Ford, O.P., traces the moment he first began to discern a call to the priesthood to a time during his young adulthood when his brother Steve asked him a question about the problem of suffering.[1]

Steve, a police officer, told Michail of an arrest he had made that morning of a man who had been systematically abusing his six-year-old stepson. The case hit Steve especially hard because he himself was the father of three young sons. "How," he asked Michail, "could I look into the eyes of that little boy and tell him that God really does love him and wants nothing but the best for him after God let that go on for so long?"

Michail was not particularly religious at that time, and the answer he gave surprised himself: "Because God sent you there to stop it from ever happening again."

■ ■ ■

Thomas Aquinas (1225–1274), the great theological master of the religious order that Michail came to enter, knew something about childhood pain and divine providence.

Known to his family as Tommaso d'Aquino, the future Doctor of the Church was five years old in 1231 when his nurse, acting on his parents' orders, took him away from his family castle in what is now southern Italy. She dropped him at the nearby Benedictine abbey of Montecassino, to be raised and educated by strangers.

For a child from a wealthy and powerful family, there was nothing abnormal about the arrangement; in fact, as Thomas's parents well knew, it was considered praiseworthy to give a son to God, even one so young. In leaving him at the prestigious abbey (along with a sizable monetary gift to the monks), his father, Landolf—a baron of Emperor Frederick II—and his mother, Theodora, had high hopes that their boy would make them proud by one day rising to the office of abbot.

Yet, knowing that Thomas was already beginning to show signs of the wisdom and holiness that would make him one of the Church's greatest saints, there is something poignant in the scene: a five-year-old boy, who was all his life surrounded by brothers and sisters, watches the heavy monastery door close behind his nurse as she leaves him with his new "family." Like Bernard of Clairvaux, Thomas is famed not only for his piety, but also for his gentleness.

It cannot have been easy for such a sensitive child to be so suddenly detached from the only world he had ever known.

However he may have felt on that "first day of school," there is no doubt that Thomas thrived at the monastery, adapting admirably to the religious life and excelling in his studies. When he was about fourteen, he was sent to continue his schooling at the University of Naples. It was there, three years later, that he made the most important decision of his life, one that was to have dramatic consequences. God was calling him not to preside over a lavishly appointed Benedictine monastery, but to be a member of a new group of vowed religious whose members supported themselves by begging barefoot in the streets: St. Dominic's Order of Preachers, otherwise known as the Dominicans.

To say that Thomas's family was unhappy about their son's new vocation is an understatement. No Aquino son was going to be a begging preacher—at least, not if his mother had any say in the matter. The Dominicans initially tried to hide Thomas by shuttling him around their Italian priories while Theodora applied personal and political pressure to convince him to return to Montecassino. However, when the family's efforts showed no signs of letting up, the Master of the Order made the decision to send Thomas to Paris, where the Aquinos' political connections would not carry so much weight.

On a May morning in 1244, Thomas and three other friars set out for Paris on foot, since the Dominicans' rule of poverty prevented them from using such luxuries as horses. A few days later, as they rested by a spring, their tranquility was disrupted by the sound of armed men on horseback. It was a squad of soldiers from King Frederick's army, dispatched at the behest of Dame Theodora to find her son and bring him home.

Two thugs grabbed Thomas and tried to rip the friar's Dominican habit off his back. However, Thomas put up such a fight that the men feared hurting him, so they let him keep his now-tattered habit as they tied him up and forced him onto a horse. He begged to be allowed to take with him a Bible and breviary (a book of daily prayers for priests and vowed religious). One of the soldiers—one who had grabbed him—grudgingly nodded, and one of the other friars handed Thomas the precious books. Thomas did not have to be told the soldier's name. It was Rinaldo d'Aquino—his own brother.

The soldiers dropped Thomas off at a nearby castle owned by the Aquino family, where Theodora was waiting. She was distressed to see that he had not given up his habit, which was now in rags. For about a year, on his mother's orders, Thomas would be held prisoner while all his family tried to make him forsake his vocation.

Thomas had been at the castle for seven months or so and was about nineteen years old when Rinaldo and another brother returned from military service. Incensed that their brother was still wearing his tattered habit and showing no sign of reneging on his Dominican vows, the men decided to take matters into their own hands. If he would not quit the Dominicans, perhaps he could be made to do something that would cause the Dominicans to quit him.

And so it was that on a cold winter's day the brothers barged into Thomas's makeshift cell to deposit a beautiful young visitor who had never before set foot in the

Aquino household—and who would likely not have been allowed in at all, had Theodora known. Thomas, sitting by a fireplace, looked up from his Bible and found himself face-to-face with a prostitute.

The next thing anyone heard was the woman's shrieks. The brothers were stunned to see her run out of the cell as Thomas waved a flaming brand. As soon as she exited—shaken but unharmed—he slammed the door behind her. Still holding the torch, he burned a cross onto the wall before weariness and fear overtook him. He fell to the ground and the tears began to flow.

As the teenage friar knelt in prayer, he fell into a deep sleep. He dreamed that angels came and girded him with a white cord of chastity. They tied it around him so tightly that he cried out in pain. As he woke up, he discovered the dream was true—the cord was really there.

Biographers usually conclude this episode by informing us that Thomas kept the story a secret until he was on his deathbed, when he revealed it to his confessor and added that he was never tempted against chastity again. By stressing that he was never again tempted, they imply that the saint reacted to the intrusion so intensely because the prostitute was truly tempting. A fourteenth-century Dominican named Bernard Gui, one of the first to chronicle Thomas's life, wrote that he was tempted but quickly controlled it.[2]

However, I don't think it was that simple—and perhaps neither did Gui, for he writes in his next sentence, "Chastity and indignation leapt up together." Gui's acknowledgment of the saint's righteous anger illuminates the fact that what Thomas's brothers did wasn't simply a temptation. It was a *violation*.

Before that incident, although he was captive, Thomas—alone in his cell, sitting by the fire in his ragged habit with his Bible and his breviary—still had his own private space. Deprived of the conversation of his fellow friars, he could at least keep up his intimate conversation with God. When his brothers invaded his inner sanctum and thrust the prostitute before him, that peace, privacy, and unobstructed intimacy were shattered.

Today we live in a sex-saturated culture, where advertisers are eager to make us believe we need to buy products in order to be wanted and do everything they can to put images of "perfect bodies" wherever we look. As a result, it takes effort to imagine a time when people could easily choose not to see things that would assault their purity. But we must make that effort if we are to understand that Thomas's brothers were not merely making him look at a pretty lady. Medieval prostitutes were required by law to dress distinctively so that a passer-by could easily identify which women were or were not for sale. So the woman whom Thomas's brothers thrust before him would have had a distinctive band or tassel on the arm of her dress. Her face would have been made up in a manner unlike any woman the youth would ever have seen.

For one so gentle as Thomas, the effect of witnessing close up a woman who had chosen or was forced to demean herself—and seeing his own brothers urge her on—would have been like being forced to watch a performance of sadomasochism. Here was the crown of creation, a beautiful human being in God's image, reduced to a painted mask—no longer a person, but a caricature, an object, a dressed-up piece of meat. The image was tragic. It was grotesque. And now it was imprinted upon Thomas's mind, put there by the perverted will of the very men who, from his childhood, were supposed to protect him.

As I imagine the saint experiencing this attack on his purity, his subsequent actions—dropping to his knees "weary and frightened, and almost despairing," and then falling asleep while praying—suddenly seem very familiar. They are familiar to anyone who suffers from post-traumatic stress disorder: all of the physical and emotional sensations that Thomas's biographers describe typically accompany a flashback.

Granted, "diagnosing" a saint according to modern-day understandings of psychology and science can easily take us off course. Sanctity comes from acceptance of God's grace, and so is necessarily supernatural—beyond anything that could be explained by natural causes. However, as I wrote when discussing St. Josephine Bakhita in chapter 1, there is a long tradition of calling saints patrons of certain physical or mental conditions not because they had those actual conditions, but because they underwent experiences *like* them. St. Thomas's physical experience places him in fellowship with those who have suffered PTSD flashbacks, even if he did not actually endure post-traumatic stress.

That said, at the time of the prostitute incident, if he were in fact vulnerable to what PTSD sufferers know as "memory triggers," Thomas had no shortage of potential triggers in his past. His family had already exposed him to neglect or abuse many times—having him dropped off at Montecassino (technically not "neglect," but it would have had the same impact on a five-year-old), abducting him, imprisoning him, and rejecting his Dominican vocation. That rejection would have been the most painful for Thomas of all the traumas, in that from his perspective—having heard a call from God to become a friar—it amounted to a denial of his very identity.

What I find particularly moving is that, regardless of whether he actually underwent a flashback, Thomas's actions in the wake of the attack provide a model for anyone who suffers such trauma. First, he permitted himself to relax. Why is that important? Because a flashback is not just in the mind, but is a full-body experience. Once the mind has revisited the emotional trauma and the adrenaline rush begins to dissipate, the sufferer can feel drained and bereft—like his or her life has been sucked out.

It may seem obvious to suggest that the best thing to do at that moment of feeling drained is to allow oneself to take time out. However, the temptation for some is to try to carry on as though nothing had happened, sucking in the pain. I speak from experience. To admit I am overwhelmed with mental and physical exhaustion is to admit I have lost control. When I realize the complete disproportion between the event that triggered my flashback and the way I reacted to it, I feel humiliated. However, it is at that moment, when I most want to pretend everything is normal, that it is essential I find a private space to rest—and, if necessary, cry it out—to prevent being eaten away by pent-up tension.

Second, and more importantly, Thomas prayed. As with taking time out to relax, opening your heart to God is a therapeutic act in and of itself, because it counters the temptation to hold pain inside. But of course, prayer is not a merely natural act, like clearing your mind or relaxing your muscles. It is a *supernatural* act, prompted by grace, and it invites supernatural help.

I wrote in chapter 3 of experiencing joy through praying amidst a flashback: "Dear Jesus, I know I can choose to suffer this with you, or without you. I choose to suffer this *with* you. Don't leave me." This kind of prayer is effective because it engages the one part of you that cannot ever be completely overwhelmed by a flashback: your will.

The flashback feels humiliating because it causes your mind and body, which normally react to stimuli in a predictable fashion, to react unpredictably. Moreover, telling yourself "There is no rational explanation why I should get so worked up about this" only gets you so far. Even if you can regain command of your reason, your body may continue its rebellion—tears flowing, heart racing—until the fight-or-flight hormones finish working their way through your system.

Yet, even in the midst of this painful loss of control, you always retain the power of willing, because you are always able to will how you accept what is happening. Your will determines whether you accept unavoidable pain with doubt or faith; with despair or hope; and with hatred or love. If you choose rightly, you will find that the very thing that causes you humiliation on one level can, on a deeper level, bring healing in Christ.

This observation about how that which humiliates us can heal us, although in my own words, is not really mine. It belongs to St. Thomas Aquinas, who speaks of it in the *Summa* when explaining why sacraments are necessary for our salvation.

A sacrament is a sign of a holy thing so far as it makes people holy. Being a sign, it is not purely spiritual; it always involves something we can see, hear, feel, taste, or touch. When explaining the necessity of the sacraments, one of the reasons Thomas offers is that people who sin do so by putting themselves under the authority of things that are not God—physical things, like wealth, food, or illicit sexual passion. "Now," Thomas says, "the healing remedy should be given to a man so as to reach the part affected by disease." So, if the disease of sin is physical, it is appropriate that God should provide us with "a spiritual medicine" by means of physical things. Conversely, if he tried to heal us by purely spiritual means, without any visible signs, we would be unable to wrap our minds around them because we are so attracted to the world of our senses.[3]

It reminds me of the story preachers like to tell about the mom who tries to get her young daughter not to be afraid to sleep with the lights out, by telling the girl that she is safe since God is with her. The girl says, "I know—but I need God with skin on." Likewise, we humans have the need to perceive something with our senses that reassures us of God's healing presence, hence the necessity of the "sensible signs" that are the sacraments.

Thomas's larger point is that such signs are healing in part because they are *humbling*. They humble us through forcing us to recognize that we have allowed ourselves to fall under the sway of physical things. Once we have that humility, God can use it to meet us where we are—taking sacraments we can sense, and in and through them conveying the healing power of his presence.

With that in mind, look at the humility of Thomas's own prayer following the attack on his purity, as he knelt weeping. He could have asked God to take charge of his circumstances, so that no one would ever again try to tempt him. But he didn't. Instead, he asked God to take charge of *him*. While an early biographer's account says he sought the gift of chastity, the version of Thomas's prayer given by a nineteenth-century Dominican is more expressive, and no less accurate: he "earnestly begged of God to accept the whole offering of his body as well as his soul."[4]

The depth of this prayer's meaning may be glimpsed through a passage that Thomas wrote nearly thirty years later, toward the end of his life. Defining chastity in his *Summa Theologiae*, he said the word could be applied in two ways. The first was the more common understanding of chastity as referring to ruling one's sexual passions, rather than allowing oneself to be ruled by them. It would have been natural for Thomas to pray for that gift when he fell to his knees after chasing away the prostitute. But I believe he also prayed for the second kind of chastity he would describe in the *Summa*: a "*spiritual* chastity."[5] Spiritual chastity is the virtue that enables you to have a deeper union with God by empowering you to withdraw from things that take you away from him. It is rooted in charity—the love of God that enables us to love our neighbors as ourselves.

At that moment when the frightened young friar knelt down clasping his ash-stained hands, still breathing the mingled scent of the prostitute's perfume and the smoke from his torch, he did not just fear lust. He feared what would happen to him if the image of what he had witnessed remained seared in his memory. If he chose to cling to anger, resentment, or anything not of God, his hard-won spiritual chastity would be lost.

We know Thomas's prayer was answered. The proof shines not only in his legendary purity, but also in the great love he showed to all who came within his orbit, including his family. After they released him from captivity, instead of shunning them, he remained close with his family for the rest of his life—visiting them during his travels and helping them in times of need. In this way, he not only fulfilled the commandment to forgive interiorly, but also lived up to what he would call the most "perfect" level of reconciliation—"where the one offended seeks out the offender."[6] Like Maria Goretti and Laura Vicuña, Thomas Aquinas is a patron saint of forgiveness.

■ ■ ■

When I announced my plans to write this book, Terry Nelson, the Catholic artist and online diarist who was sexually victimized as a young boy (see chapter 3), wrote on his website that he had long been searching for a saint who had been raped, to no avail. He had learned of numerous martyrs of chastity who were killed during or after resisting rape, but none who were actually violated.

> In the process of looking for these saints, [writes Terry,] I've reflected on the very human need we all have to understand the bad things that happened to us in life, as well as the desire to have someone understand our pain. . . . [Finding] a saint who went through the exact same terrible things we may have endured seems to me to represent a sign of hope for us that good really can come from evil. That through the blood of Christ virginity is restored, sanctity triumphs over wickedness, and so on. Hence our desire to find saints just like ourselves.[7]

Terry's thoughts moved me to see if I could succeed where he could not, in the hope that it might bring comfort to him and others. On my own, before seeking outside expertise, I too was unable to find a saint who had been raped, but I did find one who experienced a particularly humiliating form of sexual abuse. The eighteen-year-old Joan of Arc, at the time of her trial by the English, was made more than once to submit to tests at the hands of matrons to prove she was the virgin she claimed to be. Her suffering places her in fellowship with not only sexual-abuse victims, but also those who suffer ridicule over their efforts to maintain their purity.

Having exhausted my own resources, I then contacted an investigating judge for the Vatican's Congregation for the Causes of Saints to ask if there was any saint who had been violated. The official answered that certainly there were, given the accounts from St. Augustine and others of the virgin martyrs of antiquity, who were raped before being killed.

Remembering the longing that Terry felt to know of a saint who went through what he endured, and realizing there must be many others like him, I pressed the official. Could he give me *one name* of a saint who had been violated?

The official spent a few days returning to the files of some martyrs of chastity for whom he himself had been an investigating judge. He then phoned me from his office at the Vatican with the answer. It was not what I expected.

He said that he had been unable to find a saint who could be said with certainty to have been violated. However, he added, there was a twentieth-century martyr of chastity, a teenage girl, whose body when found was so decomposed that it was impossible to know for sure whether violation had occurred. Whether she was vio- lated or not, he said, did not matter with regard to the girl's sanctity. She remained a martyr of chastity for the same reason that any holy person is declared a martyr of chastity—not because she was inviolate, but because she *resisted* violation. And he told me her name: Blessed Karolina Kózka, beatified in 1987 by Pope John Paul II.

At first, I was disappointed that the official had failed to come up with the name of a saint known to have been raped. Upon reflection, however, I realized that the lack of certainty over whether Karolina was violated does not make her a less fitting patron for victims of childhood sexual abuse, but rather a more fitting one.

We victims do not normally tell all the details of what happened to us to everyone we meet. In this book, I have been upfront about some of my own experiences in the hope of helping others, but even I am not sharing every detail. If a thief broke into my bedroom, robbed it, and escaped, it would still be my bedroom; it would not automatically become public space. Likewise, the fact that my sexual sphere was invaded does not make it any less my own. It remains covered with the veil of reverence, a veil that protects both my own modesty and that of others. If the veil is to be lifted, the choice of what to disclose and how to disclose it should come from me, not from someone outside.

With that in mind, I now realize that if there were a saint whom we knew for certain was raped, our knowledge of that rape would be, in itself, a kind of intrusion into the saint's private sphere. The very mystery surrounding the question of what was or was not done to Karolina serves to protect her personal dignity. Such mystery is needed to counter the voyeuristic mentality promoted by the popular media, which broadcasts details of sexual crimes to all audiences at all hours.

And it also serves to counter the misinformed efforts of some members of the faithful who (as I wrote when discussing St. Maria Goretti in chapter 5) imply that being raped removes one from the ranks of the pure.

Some of those telling Karolina Kózka's story highlight the claim of a midwife who allegedly examined Karolina's body and said she was not violated. But, according to the Vatican official, the claim has no scientific validity, since Karolina's body was found more than two weeks after she was murdered. "We really do not know whether she was violated or not," he told me. "We have no certainty what really happened to her."

But even if the claim were true, given that all who knew Karolina testified to her purity, given that her wounds showed she put up a fierce struggle, what would it have to do with her holiness? Is she supposed to be more holy because she had the strength to fight off her attacker before he could rape her? Would a girl equally pure, but not capable of putting up such a good fight, be deprived of the martyr's crown? Of course not—yet the erroneous idea that a rape victim cannot be a martyr finds its way even to the Vatican website. The site's biography of another holy girl, Blessed Albertina Berkenbrock, who was killed while resisting an attacker, states, "Her reputation as a martyr was confirmed when the local midwife who had examined her body stated that the attempted rape was not a success."[8] No wonder the faithful are confused.

When I pointed out the claim in the Blessed Albertina biography to the Vatican official, he assured me the implication that a saint who was violated could not be a true martyr was "downright nonsense." The problem, he explained, is that some of the website's materials on saints are written by journalists who are not theologians.

"People do not always understand" what makes a saint a martyr of chastity, the official went on. "It is for this reason extremely important that these things are clarified. You can make this distinction by distinguishing clearly between bodily integrity and moral integrity."

He explained to me that there are two aspects of virginity—physiological and moral. Moral virginity is in the intellect and will. "One can be physically violated and still be a virgin in the moral sense." Since being raped does not involve consent of the will, holy people who were raped before being killed have done nothing worthy of reproach. "On the contrary," the official went on, "if they tried to defend themselves [and were yet violated], they are in a privileged position. . . . They are martyrs in *the truest possible sense*." In other words, far from being stained or impure, they are the heavenly witnesses who "have washed their robes and made them white in the blood of the Lamb" (Rev 7:14).

■ ■ ■

Karolina Kózka (1898–1914) lived and died in the Polish farming village of Wal-Ruda.⁹ The story of her short life and martyrdom, perhaps more so than any other saint in this book, demonstrates how saints attain their deepest understanding of Christ and themselves through the Eucharist. It is in receiving Christ's Body that they learn how to receive their own body, and it is in defending the dignity of Christ that they learn how to defend their own dignity.

Born on her family's farm as the fourth of eleven children, Karolina had a solid religious foundation through her parents, Jan and Maria, who instilled in her a love for the prayers of the Church. Although physically strong (she was never ill), she was emotionally sensitive, and could be deeply troubled when noticing her own failures.

After her death, friends recalled Karolina as being generous, kind, and sympathetic. But they also remembered her as "ordinary"—not drawing undue attention to herself. One of her peers said, "Karolina was better than us: more hard-working, more pious, more sacrificial, more assiduous. She did the same things as others, but better and more."

Like Maria Goretti and Laura Vicuña, she loved formal prayer, but Karolina's devotion expressed itself in her entire attitude. Conversation with God was natural for her; she prayed not because she was supposed to but because she wanted to. Prayer fulfilled a deep longing of her heart. She also conversed with the Blessed Mother, sometimes becoming lost in devotion as she arranged flowers before the family's Mary statue. But the most outstanding quality by far in Karolina's life of faith was her Eucharistic devotion. Friends said she loved the hymn sung during the Corpus Christi procession, "Zróbcie Mu Miejsce" ("Make Room for Him"), making its words the theme of her life:

> Make room for him: the Lord is coming from heaven!
> Concealed in the form of Bread. . . .
>
> He is giving us gifts at home and in the fields.
> He only demands the sacrifice of our hearts.

> We are bringing them to you, God! We are bring-
>   ing them!
> Give us graces, we are giving you our hearts.
>
> And the witnesses of this exchange between parties
> Will be heaven and the earth.[10]

To her peers, Karolina's love of the Blessed Sacrament seemed eccentric at times. Before Mass one morning on the Feast of Corpus Christi, a day on which the Eucharist was to be carried in procession, while other girls were busy putting on their Sunday best, Karolina was following the hymn's direction to "make room for him." She went to the footpaths surrounding the church, removing dry grass or lumps of soil. When a friend asked what she was doing, she said, "Today Lord Jesus passes through the fields; it should be clean and neat everywhere."

Given her personal affection for the Eucharistic Lord, I am not surprised to learn that, after receiving Holy Communion, Karolina would kneel in her pew and recite the *Anima Christi* by heart (see chapter 1). It is the prayer of a soul who seeks union: "Within thy wounds, hide me / Never permit me to be separated from thee . . ." I feel a kinship with her, knowing that she, like me, longed to be "hidden with Christ in God" (Col 3:3 NAB), surrounded by his protective love and mercy.

On the last day of her life, November 18, 1914, sixteen-year-old Karolina begged to accompany her mother to church, but was ordered to stay inside because it was too dangerous. World War I had begun; Wal-Ruda had been taken over by the Russian army, and rumors were rampant that the Cossacks were abducting local girls.

While Maria was at Mass, a large, threatening Cossack invaded the Kózka home. He grabbed Karolina's father and shook him, demanding to know where the Austrian armies were. Then he saw Karolina. Screaming and swearing, accusing the father and daughter of hiding information, he ordered them to go with him to his commanding officer. Karolina and Jan had to march ahead of the soldier, a bayonet at their backs.

As they approached the forest, Jan, fearing for his daughter, tried to direct the soldier toward the village instead. This only infuriated the soldier, who ordered the father to return home, threatening him with death if he disobeyed. Jan lingered a moment in shock and fear, and then reluctantly turned back. That was the last he ever saw of his daughter.

A short while later, as Jan stood leaning against the corner of his barn, crying and looking at the forest, two local teenage boys ran in his direction. They had been hiding in the forest when they saw a woman whom they did not recognize struggling against a large soldier. Seeing Jan in such a state, the boys realized that the woman they had seen was Karolina. So they told him what they had seen: she was defending herself bravely against the assailant and had even managed to run some distance from him.

It was not until December 4, more than two weeks later, that Karolina's body was found lying face up in a bog, amongst alder trees coated in the season's first snow. Her eyes were open and turned to the sky. Her arms and chest displayed bayonet wounds. Barefoot, her muddied legs were scratched with thorns of blackberries and hawthorns through which she had forced her way in her effort to escape. In her struggle, she had run some distance from where the boys had spotted her. Her murderer was never caught.

■ ■ ■

The stories of Maria Goretti and Laura Vicuña's martyrdoms are intertwined with poignant tales of forgiveness. The saints' charity seems to merge with their chastity. In Karolina's death, I see her efforts to defend herself from rape, but I have no knowledge of what transpired between her and her attacker. What is it about her that makes me so certain her resistance was more than a mere act of self-defense—that it was, in fact, an act of the highest love?

The answer for me is the same as it was for Maria Goretti, Laura Vicuña, and all the martyrs of chastity. It is in the way Karolina's Eucharistic devotion formed her entire understanding of spirit and flesh. To be a martyr is never to die for the sake of one's own interest. St. Paul, writing at a time of martyrdom, told the persecuted Roman church, "None of us lives to himself, and none of us dies to himself" (Rom 14:7). So to say that Karolina, or any martyr of chastity, died defending "her" chastity is misleading. She was not only defending her own chastity, but also mine and yours. And she was not only defending physical chastity, but also *spiritual* chastity—the chastity that Thomas Aquinas linked with charity, which brings us into union with God and one another. Because she knew what it meant to have Christ within her, she knew that the body is the temple of the Holy Spirit. It was in defense of the sanctity of that temple—the sanctity of *all* our bodies—that she resisted unto death. That is why John Paul II said in his homily at her beatification, "Karolina didn't save her earthly life. . . . She gave it away in order to gain living with Christ in God. . . . Falling under an assailant's hand on this earth, Karolina, for the last time, bore witness to this life which is in her since the moment of baptism."[11]

We are all witnesses.

■ ■ ■

I was not the first person in my family to experience childhood trauma, although I hope to God that I am the last. On two occasions as a young teenager, my mother endured long weeks without her own mother, when my Grandma Jessie was hospitalized for nervous breakdowns. During the second hospitalization, my Grandpa Buddy, desolate and exhausted with the responsibilities of caring for five children, sat down at the dining-room table and poured out a poem titled "Shalom." When my grandmother returned home, she was so touched by it that she wrote it out in her beautiful calligraphy, framed it, and hung it on the dining-room wall. Its first stanza reads,

> Dear God, my prayer's a simple one
> Teach me the meaning of "Shalom"
> that perfect peace may come to me
> for days that passed, and days to be.[12]

I have read that poem hundreds of times since my earliest childhood, and it is only at this moment that I notice my grandfather's request for a "perfect peace" not just for the present and future, but for "days that passed."

In the Extraordinary Form of the Roman Rite (the Latin Mass whose language formed the spirituality of the saints in this book), at the end of the Lord's Prayer the priest makes a petition that begins, "Deliver us, we beg you, Lord, from every evil, past, present, and to come." In fact, if I omit the names of the saints mentioned in the prayer, it reads remarkably like my grandfather's poem:

> Deliver us, we beg you, Lord,
> from every evil, past, present, and to come; . . .
> Grant, of your goodness, peace in our days,
> that aided by the riches of your mercy,
> we may be always free from sin
> and safe from all disturbance.[13]

What did my grandfather know that the authors of the Church's liturgy also knew? How can we ask God for the peace that delivers us from the evils of the *past*?

I suspect what my grandfather knew was that God transcends time. In his faith, he believed divine providence could tie up the loose ends of his life so that even the most tangled knots and frayed edges of his past could become part of a gorgeous tapestry.

In the prayer of the Mass, I see that same divine transcendence and providence, but there is something more. The priest prays for deliverance from past, present, and future evils as he holds the paten containing the consecrated Host. Through the Eucharist, not only is my present and future life "hidden with Christ," but my past as well. The evil of my past is still evil, but it no longer has any power over me. All that remains of it are my wounds. Now I can look at the Crucified One—broken like me—as the priest holds the Host, and those same wounds become a point of entrance for his body, blood, soul, and divinity. *Domine, non sum dignus*—"Lord, I am not worthy . . ."

■ ■ ■

My friend Drusilla, a Catholic orphan who was subjected to brutal abuse by her foster father and siblings, felt as a child that she had been "thrown to the wolves." "I had to pretend to be a wolf so as to keep myself from being torn to pieces," she writes in her online journal.

> I even wrote a short story entitled *The Wolf-Cat*, wherein a young kitten, whose pride has been killed by wolves, hides in the skin of a dead wolf so that she will be taken in by the pack and not left alone to die. She is used and abused, treated the way the wolves (in my story at least) treat their kind, until the day comes when the big Cat calls her back to herself, restores her memory and tells her that she has a mission to help him save the wolves.[14]

Today, Drusilla seeks to bring that same happy ending to her own story:

> I no longer live with the wolves. I am a cat once again and happy to be one. But I have not forgotten my time in a wolf's skin. At times I still feel shame, feel I deserve to be abused, feel I deserve to be in hell—fire is very attractive. But in Jesus' wounds I remember that the flames burned me but never owned me. I belong to Christ and I never want to belong to anyone else. . . .
>
> I know the way out of hell and it is my job to tell others how to reach safety. It's not an exalted mission by any means. It mostly consists in befriending those God brings into my life, praying for those in need and most especially for victims of abuse and for those who abused them. It's nothing terribly exciting

unless being a klaxon horn is exciting. I just tell
those being burned that there is a sure way out
of the flames, that way is Jesus.[15]

Two years ago, when I first read Michail Ford's story
of how he discerned his priestly vocation, the question
that was posed to him by his brother Steve—as well as
Michail's answer—affected me deeply. Steve, thinking of
the six-year-old who was abused by his stepfather, had
asked, "How could I look into the eyes of that little boy
and tell him that God really does love him . . . ?" That, I
realized, was the very question that haunted me in my
own life: If I were to meet my younger, abused self—the
little girl who still lives inside my memory—how could I
look into her eyes and tell her God really does love her?

Michail's answer was that God, in his love, sent Steve
to rescue that boy. What was my answer? God had rescued
me, bringing me into the faith so that I might share in his
divine life. He took a bit longer to do it than in the case
of the six-year-old boy—twenty-five years longer, to be
exact—but he did it. That is proof enough of his love. But
on its own that answer still somehow wasn't enough to
make me capable of living with the memories of my abuse
and the wounds it caused.

So I kept pondering the question, and I have been pondering it prayerfully throughout the writing of this book,
hoping to find an answer in the light of Christ. And I think
I have found one. In essence, it is the same as the one that
came to Drusilla.

God permitted my heart to be wounded so that I might
take shelter in Jesus' pierced Heart, and so that Jesus might
find a home in mine. But, beyond even that, he permitted
it so that my heart would be big enough to provide shelter

to other wounded souls, bringing to them the same Christ I have received.

That, I realize, is what the saints have done for me all through my journey; they opened their hearts to me so that I might, through their love, enter more deeply into the Heart of Christ. It is the mission of the entire Communion of Saints—that we may all be one, even as the Father and the Son are one (Jn 17:11). In his will is our peace.[16]

Reader's Guide

Designed for individuals as well as reading groups, this guide includes discussion questions and prayers referenced in the text.

Discussion Questions for Reading Groups

Meeting One—Introduction through Chapter 4

1. Before reading *My Peace I Give You*, did you know there were saints who suffered childhood sexual abuse, or are you surprised? If you had heard of such saints, which ones had you heard about? If you are surprised, why is news of such saints surprising?

2. St. Josephine Bakhita gained an appreciation of divine providence through seeing how God brought good out of evil. Tell about a time in your life when what seemed like God's worst for you turned out to be his best.

3. In chapter 2, the author talks about a trio of stained-glass windows that helped her gain deeper insight into the meaning of the Sacred Heart devotion. Has a holy image or statue helped you in your own spiritual walk? Where did you see it, and what did it mean for you?

4. Who comes to mind—perhaps a friend, family member, or saint—when you think of someone who shared in Christ's Passion?

5. How does St. Thérèse of Lisieux help us to understand the difference between literal childhood and spiritual childhood?

Meeting Two—Chapters 5 through 8

1. Blessed Laura Vicuña is often called "another Maria
    Goretti." What are some notable similarities between
    her witness and that of Maria? What are some notable
    differences?

2. Dorothy Day found fulfillment not only in biological
    motherhood, but in spiritual motherhood as well. Who
    has been a spiritual mother or father to you? To whom
    have you been a spiritual mother or father?

3. God has not permitted Blessed Margaret of Castel-
    lo's body to suffer corruption. What does his choice
    to preserve this physically deformed saint say to our
    culture's obsession with youth and beauty?

4. Read the first three paragraphs of chapter 8 out loud.
    What emotions are brought up for you by the story of
    Michail Ford, O.P., and his brother Steve? How would
    you have responded if Steve asked you the question
    he asked Michail ("How could I look into the eyes of
    that little boy and tell him that God really does love
    him . . .")?

5. When you receive Christ in the Eucharist, you com-
    mune with the One who was in the beginning, is now,
    and ever shall be. If you were to truly internalize this
    truth, how would this contact with the eternal God
    affect your appreciation of the day-to-day events of
    your life? (Think of Dorothy Day's comment in chapter
    6, for example, where she says she could not accom-
    plish her work without the "constant reassurance"
    provided by the Mass.)

Prayers

Anima Christi

Soul of Christ, sanctify me.
Body of Christ, save me.
Blood of Christ, inebriate me.
Water from Christ's side, wash me.
Passion of Christ, strengthen me.
O good Jesus, hear me.
Within Thy wounds hide me.
Suffer me not to be separated from Thee.
From the malicious enemy defend me.
In the hour of my death call me.
And bid me come unto Thee,
That I may praise Thee with Thy saints
and with Thy angels,
Forever and ever.
Amen.

The Litany of the Sacred Heart of Jesus

Lord, have mercy.
Christ, have mercy.
Lord, have mercy.
Christ, graciously hear us.
God, the Father of Heaven, have mercy on us.
God, the Son, Redeemer of the World, have mercy on us.
God, the Holy Ghost, have mercy on us.
Holy Trinity, one God, have mercy on us.
Heart of Jesus, Son of the Eternal Father, have mercy on us.
Heart of Jesus, formed in the womb of the Virgin Mother by the Holy Ghost, have mercy on us.

Heart of Jesus, united substantially with the word of God, have mercy on us.

Heart of Jesus, of infinite majesty, have mercy on us.

Heart of Jesus, holy temple of God, have mercy on us.

Heart of Jesus, tabernacle of the Most High, have mercy on us.

Heart of Jesus, house of God and gate of heaven, have mercy on us.

Heart of Jesus, glowing furnace of charity, have mercy on us.

Heart of Jesus, vessel of justice and love, have mercy on us.

Heart of Jesus, full of goodness and love, have mercy on us.

Heart of Jesus, abyss of all virtues, have mercy on us.

Heart of Jesus, most worthy of all praise, have mercy on us.

Heart of Jesus, king and center of all hearts, have mercy on us.

Heart of Jesus, in whom are all the treasures of wisdom and knowledge, have mercy on us.

Heart of Jesus, in whom dwelleth all the fullness of the Divinity, have mercy on us.

Heart of Jesus, in whom the Father is well pleased, have mercy on us.

Heart of Jesus, of whose fullness we have all received, have mercy on us.

Heart of Jesus, desire of the everlasting hills, have mercy on us.

Heart of Jesus, patient and rich in mercy, have mercy on us.

Heart of Jesus, rich to all who invoke Thee, have mercy on us.

Heart of Jesus, fount of life and holiness, have mercy on us.

Heart of Jesus, propitiation for our sins, have mercy on us.

Heart of Jesus, saturated with revilings, have mercy on us.

Heart of Jesus, crushed for our iniquities, have mercy on us.

Heart of Jesus, made obedient unto death, have mercy on us.

Heart of Jesus, pierced with a lance, have mercy on us.

Heart of Jesus, source of all consolation, have mercy on us.

Heart of Jesus, our life and resurrection, have mercy on us.

Heart of Jesus, our peace and reconciliation, have mercy on us.

Heart of Jesus, victim for our sins, have mercy on us.

Heart of Jesus, salvation of those who hope in Thee, have mercy on us.

Heart of Jesus, hope of those who die in Thee, have mercy on us.

Heart of Jesus, delight of all saints, have mercy on us.

Lamb of God, who takest away the sins of the world, spare us, O Lord.

Lamb of God, who takest away the sins of the world, graciously hear us, O Lord,

Lamb of God who takest away the sins of the world, have mercy on us.

V. Jesus, meek and humble of Heart.

R. Make our hearts like unto Thine.

Let us pray

Almighty and everlasting God, look upon the Heart
of Thy well-beloved Son and upon the acts of praise
and satisfaction which He renders unto Thee in the
name of sinners; and do Thou, in Thy great goodness, grant pardon to them who seek Thy mercy, in
the name of the same Thy Son, Jesus Christ, who
liveth and reigneth with Thee, world without end.

Te Deum

O God, we praise Thee, and acknowledge Thee to be
the supreme Lord.

Everlasting Father, all the earth worships Thee.

All the Angels, the heavens and all angelic powers,

All the Cherubim and Seraphim, continuously cry to
Thee:

Holy, Holy, Holy, Lord God of Hosts!

Heaven and earth are full of the Majesty of Thy glory.

The glorious choir of the Apostles,

The wonderful company of Prophets,

The white-robed army of Martyrs, praise Thee.

Holy Church throughout the world acknowledges
Thee:

The Father of infinite Majesty;

Thy adorable, true and only Son;

Also the Holy Spirit, the Comforter.

O Christ, Thou art the King of glory!

Thou art the everlasting Son of the Father.

When Thou tookest it upon Thyself to deliver man,

Thou didst not disdain the Virgin's womb.

Having overcome the sting of death, Thou opened the
Kingdom of Heaven to all believers.

Thou sittest at the right hand of God in the glory of
the Father.
We believe that Thou willst come to be our Judge.
We, therefore, beg Thee to help Thy servants whom
Thou hast redeemed with Thy Precious Blood.
Let them be numbered with Thy Saints in everlasting
glory.

V. Save Thy people, O Lord, and bless Thy inheritance!
R. Govern them, and raise them up forever.

V. Every day we thank Thee.
R. And we praise Thy Name forever, yes, forever and
ever.

V. O Lord, deign to keep us from sin this day.
R. Have mercy on us, O Lord, have mercy on us.

V. Let Thy mercy, O Lord, be upon us, for we have
hoped in Thee.
R. O Lord, in Thee I have put my trust; let me never
be put to shame.

Shalom
(Written by my grandfather)

Dear God, my prayer's a simple one
Teach me the meaning of "Shalom"
that perfect peace may come to me
for days that passed, and days to be.

Give love of honest work to do
Then peace when needed tasks are through,
great calm that rests and sweet repose
when sun has set and shadows close.

Direct our hands to do their best
to shield the weak, help the oppressed
Strengthen their faith and ours renew
Better the world that we first knew.

And give us all that greatest love
that we may grow and rise above
all senseless feuds and petty spite
and light our lives with radiant light.

And lead us to that perfect peace
when strife shall end and envy cease,
when all shall join in unity
Dear God, make "Shalom" real to me.

—Bud, 1955

Further Reading

St. Josephine Bakhita

Maynard, Jean Owen. *Josephine Bakhita: The Lucky One*. London: Catholic Truth Society, 2002.

Mary

Sheen, Fulton J. *The World's First Love*. San Francisco: Ignatius Press, 1996 (originally published 1952).

Gemma Galgani

Sr. Saint Michael. *Portrait of St. Gemma*. New York: P.J. Kennedy & Sons, 1949 (out of print).

A website maintained by an admirer of Gemma gives recommendations of other books on the saint: www.st gemmagalgani.com/2008/10/books-on-st-gemma-galgani .html.

Thérèse of Lisieux

Gaucher, Guy. *The Passion of Thérèse of Lisieux*. New York: Crossroad, 2006.

Maria Goretti

Poage, Godfrey, C.P. *St. Maria Goretti: In Garments All Red*. Rockford, IL: TAN Books & Publishing, 1998.

Also recommended: *Fourteen Flowers of Pardon* video documentary produced by the Mercy Foundation, available from www.ewtnreligiouscatalogue.com.

Laura Vicuña

I was unable to locate a comprehensive English-language biography of Laura that is currently in print or available in US libraries. Most of the biographical information I used was drawn from an article by John Cussen, "La Beata Laura Vicuña: The Nun's Version, Corrective of García Márquez's," *Religion and the Arts* 11.

Dorothy Day

Day, Dorothy. *The Long Loneliness*. New York: HarperOne, 1981.

Many of Dorothy's writings are available on the Catholic Worker website, www.catholicworker.org/dorothyday /index.cfm.

Bernard of Clairvaux

Bernard's *Commentary on the Song of Songs* and *On Loving God* are both available online at www.pathsoflove.com /Bernard.

Maximilian Kolbe

The best source for Maximilian's own writings is the online bookstore at www.marytown.com, the website of the National Shrine of St. Maximilian Kolbe. My favorite book about him is Patricia Treece's oral biography *A Man for Others* (Libertyville, IL: Marytown Press, 1982).

Margaret of Castello

Bonniwell, William, O.P. *The Life of Blessed Margaret of Castello, 1287–1320*. Rockford, IL: TAN Books & Publishing, 2009.

Thomas Aquinas

Chesterton, G. K. *Saint Thomas Aquinas/Saint Francis of Assisi*. San Francisco: Ignatius Press, 2002.

Resources

By a directive of the United States Conference of Catholic Bishops, every diocese and eparchy in the United States is required to address the pastoral needs of those who have been sexually abused by clergy, religious, or employees of Catholic institutions.[1] However, as this book goes to press, there is as yet no similarly organized effort among US bishops to reach out to *all* Catholic victims of sexual abuse. It is my hope that such an effort will be made in the future. For the time being, in the absence of institutional guidance, it is not easy to locate reputable resources for healing that are consistent with the Catholic faith.

The choice of organizations and websites listed in this guide reflects my judgment, at the time of this writing, of those resources that appear to be good starting points for those seeking help. Victims are encouraged to use discernment when consulting any such list, as organizations, websites, and the people behind them can change. I intend to revise these listings according to feedback from victims and those who minister to them. Please visit http://mypeace.dawneden.com for the latest updates, and send any recommendations for improving this guide to me at mypeace.dawneden@gmail.com.

Spiritual Direction

Beyond prayer and participation in the Church's sacramental life, the most important resources for Catholics seeking healing from the effects of childhood sexual abuse are a good spiritual director and a good therapist (one who is Catholic or at least respects the faith). Get both types of help if you can. If you have violent or self-destructive thoughts, or if your psychological state prevents you from functioning, the search for a therapist should come first. However, if you are not a danger to yourself or others, are handling your daily responsibilities adequately, and just need help dealing with past pain, finding a spiritual director is a greater priority.

Does a spiritual director have to be a priest? Pope Benedict XVI recommends that the faithful seek spiritual direction from "a guide reliable in doctrine and expert in the things of God," which would seem to imply choosing a priest if one is available.[2] I would add that choosing a priest over a lay spiritual director is also safer: whereas lay spiritual directors answer only to themselves, priests are required by canon law, as well as the regulations of their diocese or religious order, to observe certain norms in interacting with the faithful. (This is especially true with respect to confidentiality. If you seek direction within the context of confession, the priest cannot break the confessional seal, lest he incur automatic excommunication.)

Moreover, receiving direction from a priest affords you the opportunity to receive the Sacrament of Penance during your session. If you choose to do this, you can receive direction during your confession, or authorize the priest to discuss certain material from your confession with you during direction. (If he does, he is still bound to keep the seal of confession.) I usually confess at the beginning of my session. Then, following absolution, I give my director context on a sin I have confessed, so that he may advise me on how to deal with the temptation to commit such a sin when it comes up in the future. In my experience, receiving such direction while in a post-confession state of grace better enables me to correct the behaviors and lines of thinking that lead me to sin.

If a priest is not available, a wise vowed member of a religious order (e.g., a friar, monk, or nun) may provide spiritual direction. However, it is not a good idea to receive direction from a layperson not under vows, as the level of training given in spiritual-direction courses for the laity is far lighter than what priests or most vowed religious receive. Given the complexity of the challenges you face as a survivor of sexual abuse, the caretaker of your soul should have graduate-level training in theology and years of experience in pastoral care.

Does it cost money? Priests and vowed religious are not supposed to charge a fee for spiritual direction, but they can accept donations, and you may wish to offer, if your director has been helpful to you. (An exception is if the spiritual director is a licensed therapist who directs you within the course of providing therapy. In that case, he may discuss with you a schedule of charges, to be agreed upon mutually.)

How do I find a spiritual director? I have had the most success finding a director through contacting a local community of male vowed religious, such as the Dominicans or Capuchins. In many such communities, spiritual direction is part of their charism; moreover, their priests tend to have more time to give direction than do priests in parishes. Another option is to ask your pastor for leads on finding a spiritual director. For instance, he may know of a retired priest who has the time and energy to direct a soul.

If all else fails and you cannot find even a theologically knowledgeable vowed religious who is not a priest, find a regular confessor and confess to him at least once a month (twice is better if you can manage it). At the beginning of your confession, after saying how long it has been since your last confession, add, "And I would like some spiritual direction." (It's good to give him a heads-up that you are seeking more participation on his end than in the usual confession.) Then, as you confess your sins, point out to him which sin is particularly tied to an area of anxiety, weakness, or pain about which you need direction. While you will not have the luxury of time that you would have in a spiritual-direction session, the benefits will be similar, particularly as you continue to return to the same confessor.

What should I look for in a spiritual director? The *Catholic Encyclopedia* advises that a director be knowledgeable about the spiritual life and faithful to the magisterium of the Church.[3] In addition, it says he should help the directee deepen his or her practice of prayer and mortification (the latter being a manner of asceticism by which the soul is trained to live virtuously). Questions that may help you gauge whether a potential director fulfills these criteria include the following: What books does he recommend to directees? Does he adhere to Church teachings on marriage and sexuality? Does he work with ministries that promote those teachings, such as Courage (which helps homosexuals live chaste lives) and Project Rachel (which helps women find post-abortion healing and reconciliation)?

Another important question to ask is whether the potential director is willing to help you work out issues relating to childhood sexual abuse. I learned this the hard way after I sought out a priest for direction at a time when

I needed help dealing with other issues. After several sessions, when he had helped me with the problems that were my initial concern, I sought to bring my childhood sexual abuse into the discussion. To my surprise, the priest informed me he did not feel qualified to direct me in that area. While I appreciated his honesty, I wished I had asked the right questions at the outset to have been spared the trouble of switching spiritual directors.

What are the benefits of spiritual direction? Pope Benedict XVI has said of spiritual direction, "To go towards the Lord we always need a guide, a dialogue. We cannot do it with our thoughts alone."[4] Benedict says that such a guide will bring you to profound knowledge of yourself, leading you to a deeper union with the Lord so that "[your] life may be in ever closer conformity with the Gospel."[5]

In my own experience, I have found that a good spiritual director also helps me see my everyday challenges, anxieties, and triumphs in light of God's larger plan for my life. He encourages me by showing how God is using my personal struggles to perfect me.

Therapy

Should I choose a Catholic therapist over a non-Catholic one? The choice is up to you, but based on my own experience (see chapter 6), all other things being equal, I would recommend it.

If you choose a non-Catholic therapist and are a single person, don't be afraid to question the therapist to ensure he or she will respect your decision to live chastely. If the therapist believes that your choice for chastity necessarily reflects repression, fear of sex, or irrational submission to authority, go elsewhere. (This is not to deny that some victims of childhood sexual abuse may indeed be repressed or afraid of sex. However, a good therapist should not consider chastity itself to be evidence of pathology.)

Another question to ask is whether the therapist is willing to consult with your spiritual director. Having your therapist and spiritual director work together can greatly aid your healing. A good therapist should have no objection to doing so with your permission.

Where can I find a Catholic therapist? The branch of Catholic Charities in your area may be able to help you find one. Visit www.catholiccharitiesusa.org to find the office of the nonprofit nearest you. The privately run website CatholicTherapists.com offers a national directory of Catholic therapists. Prominent Catholic therapy practices include the Pennsylvania-based Institute for Marital Healing, which operates MaritalHealing.com and ChildHealing.com, and the Virginia-based Alpha Omega Clinics (www.aoccs.org).

Some Catholic psychotherapy practices are led by members of lay movements such as Opus Dei and Regnum Christi. It is helpful to inquire whether a potential therapist belongs to a lay movement, as this gives insight into the manner in which the therapist practices his or her faith.

What should I look for in a therapist? Certainly you want one who is licensed in your state. Check with the state's licensing website to make sure there are no complaints against the therapist. If the name of the school the therapist attended is unfamiliar to you, search online to ensure that it is accredited. (I once had a bad experience with a therapist who called himself "Dr." When I complained to the state licensing board, they informed me his doctorate came from a diploma mill.)

Many of the same questions that should be asked of a potential spiritual director (see above) should be asked of a potential therapist as well. If the therapist works with Project Rachel or other post-abortion ministries, consider this a positive sign, as post-abortive women suffer from many of the same psychological issues as victims of childhood sexual abuse. In addition, ask specifically about the extent of the therapist's experience in the areas of childhood sexual abuse and post-traumatic stress disorder.

What should I expect from therapy? Expect to develop better coping mechanisms to handle stress and anxiety, and to learn how to counter the negative self-talk that can foster depression. A good therapist will also help you improve your interpersonal communication skills (particularly with family members and others close to you) and overcome social fears.

Organizations and Websites

As of this writing, there is no informational clearinghouse for Catholic victims of childhood sexual abuse. However, in addition to the websites noted above (www.catholic charitiesusa.org, CatholicTherapists.com, MaritalHealing .com, ChildHealing.com, and www.aoccs.org), a few Catholic organizations offer help for those seeking healing from sexual wounds:

- The **Angelic Warfare Confraternity** (www .angelicwarfare.org), an official apostolate of the Dominican Order, is, in the words of its website, "a supernatural fellowship of men and women bound to one another in love and dedicated to

pursuing and promoting chastity together under
the powerful patronage of St. Thomas Aquinas
and the Blessed Virgin Mary." I am a member and
highly recommend it, as it plugs you into a kind
of "prayer pipeline," joining you spiritually not
only to fellow members, but also with the entire
Dominican Order, which prays specifically for the
confraternity.

- **Courage** (www.couragerc.org) ministers to Catholics with same-sex attraction and their loved ones
  and is endorsed by the Pontifical Council for the
  Family. Its website states, "By developing an interior life of chastity, which is the universal call to all
  Christians, one can move beyond the confines of
  the homosexual identity to a more complete one
  in Christ."

- Founded by EWTN *Faith and Family* radio host
  Steve Wood, **St. Joseph's Covenant Keepers**
  (www.dads.org) is "a movement that seeks to
  transform society through the transformation of
  fathers and families." Its website includes a wealth
  of information on marriage, family, sexuality, and
  healing, including advice on finding and choosing
  a therapist.

- The website of the **12-Step Review** (www.12-step
  -review.org) features writings on recovery by Fr.
  Emmerich Vogt, O.P., who brings a much-needed
  Catholic perspective to the Twelve Steps pioneered
  by Alcoholics Anonymous. Friends of mine speak
  highly of Vogt's recorded talks, which are available
  through the site. However, the 12-Step Review's
  public relations leaves something to be desired:
  two e-mails sent to Vogt at the address given for
  him on the website received no reply.

- At **HealedByTruth.com**, Carrie Bucalo, a Catholic survivor of childhood sexual abuse, offers advice based on her personal journey of recovery, drawing heavily from the Carmelite mystical tradition. I was touched by some of her insights, especially those on becoming joined to "the memories of God" (www.healedbytruth.com/The_Spiritual _Journey.html).

There are also several non-Catholic websites offering helpful resources, which unfortunately are mixed with material promoting views of human sexuality and the human person that are contrary to the faith:

- The Online Help Center of the informational clearinghouse **Stop It Now!** (www.stopitnow.com) includes information for adult survivors, including advice for those who fear that their abuser remains in a position to harm children.

- Another informational clearinghouse, **Childhelp** (www.childhelp.org), sponsors the 24-hour National Child Abuse Hotline (1-800-4-A-CHILD) for reporting abuse.

- The website **National Center for PTSD** (www .ptsd.va.gov), operated by the Department of Veterans Affairs, includes a wealth of background on post-traumatic stress disorder, as well as advice on finding and choosing a therapist.

Books

- The best resource I have found on post-traumatic stress disorder is *Traumatic Stress: The Effects of Overwhelming Experience on Mind, Body, and Society*, edited by van der Kolk, MacFarlane, and Weiseath

(New York: Guilford Press, 1996; paperback edition, 2007). It is a collection of essays by experts, written in language that is, for the most part, understandable to an educated layperson.

• In my own healing journey, I was profoundly helped by M. Scott Peck's *People of the Lie: The Hope for Healing Human Evil* (New York: Simon & Schuster, 1983). Through it, I began to realize the extent to which abuse had affected me and learn how to act from my wellness rather than from my brokenness.

• Three classics by Fulton J. Sheen also helped me heal: *Peace of Soul* (1949) and *Lift Up Your Heart* (1950)—both reprinted by Triumph Books—and *Calvary and the Mass* (1936), reprinted by IVE Press. Read both *Peace of Soul* and *Lift Up Your Heart* if you want to get the most out of spiritual direction as well as therapy. It was Sheen's brilliant grasp of human psychology that spurred me to study the theology of his intellectual guide, St. Thomas Aquinas. *Calvary and the Mass* is a brief yet extraordinarily powerful work drawing upon the structure and prayers of the Mass to explain Catholic theology on redemptive suffering.

• Sheen also wrote the best book available on human sexuality written for a popular audience, *Three to Get Married* (1951), reprinted by Scepter Publishers. Nearly thirty years before his fellow Thomist Pope John Paul II gave his "Catechesis on Human Love" (popularly known as the theology of the body), Sheen took a remarkably similar approach to encapsulating Church teachings: showing how the Triune God inscribes the vocation of love in man and woman.

Notes

Foreword

1. Sr. Mary Ada, "Limbo," in *The Mary Book*, ed. F.J. Sheed, (New York: Sheed & Ward, 1950), 181-183.

Introduction

1. My sister, who is five years older than me, was not present at the times that I recall being molested or exposed to sexual inappropriateness.

2. My mother does express sorrow over my having painful memories, and has apologized for certain things, such as allowing her boyfriends to be nude in my presence. "I was not a perfect mother," she writes today, "but I did the best I could."

3. St. Augustine, *City of God*, trans. Marcus Dods, in *Nicene and Post-Nicene Fathers*, First Series, vol. 2., ed. Philip Schaff (Buffalo, NY: Christian Literature Publishing Co., 1887), Book I, chapter 18.

4. See the Reader's Guide on page 185 for the full text of the *Anima Christi*.

5. The Litany of the Sacred Heart. See the Reader's Guide on pages 185–188 for the full text.

6. See "Adverse Childhood Experiences (ACE) Study: Data and Statistics," www.cdc.gov/ace/prevalence.htm.

7. There are differing views over whether it is best to refer to people who have suffered abuse as "victims" or "survivors." Some prefer "survivors," because they see it as empowering. However, there are trauma experts who hold that calling those who have suffered abuse "survivors" can complicate healing, because it glosses over what was done to them—after all, they survived. Calling them "victims" validates their experience and

forces society to face the evil they endured. I will generally refer to them as victims.

8. Bessel A. van der Kolk, "The Complexity of Adaptation to Trauma," in *Traumatic Stress: The Effects of Overwhelming Experience on Mind, Body, and Society*, van der Kolk, ed. Bessel A. et al. (New York: Guilford Press, 1996; paperback edition, 2007), 200.

9. Fulton J. Sheen, *The Eternal Galilean* (Garden City, NY: Garden City Books, 1950 [originally published 1934]), 216.

10. Benedict XVI, General Audience, May 18, 2011, www.vatican .va/holy_father/benedict_xvi/audiences/2011/documents /hf_ben-xvi_aud_20110518_en.html.

Chapter 1: The Love We Forget

1. St. Ignatius Loyola, *Autobiography of St. Ignatius*, ed. J.F.X. O'Conor (New York: Benziger Bros., 1900), www.gutenberg.org /files/24534/24534-h/24534-h.htm.

2. *The New Raccolta* (Philadelphia: Peter Cunningham & Son, 1903), 60. Accessed online at books.google.com.

3. Second Vatican Council, *Gaudium et Spes*, 22.

4. John Paul II, *Novo Millenio Ineunte*, 8.

5. Joseph Cardinal Ratzinger, *Seek That Which Is Above* (San Francisco: Ignatius Press, 2007), 15.

6. "Josephine Bakhita," www.vatican.va/news_services /liturgy/saints/ns_lit_doc_20001001_giuseppina-bakhita _en.html.

7. Benedict XVI, *Spe Salvi*, 3.

8. Jean Maynard, *Josephine Bakhita: The Lucky One* (London: Catholic Truth Society, 2002), 5.

9. Ibid., 10.

10. Ibid., 11.

11. John N. Briere and Diana M. Elliott, "Immediate and Long-Term Impacts of Child Sexual Abuse," *The Future of Children*, #4, no. 2, Center for the Future of Children, David and Lucille Packard Foundation, Sexual Abuse of Children (Summer-Autumn, 1994): #58.

12. John Paul II, "Letter to Families," 8.

13. Ibid., 11.

14. Ibid., 12.

15. Ibid., 14, 8.

16. Molly Jong-Fast, *Girl [Maladjusted]* (New York: Villard Books, 2006), 83.

17. Karol Wojtyla, *Love and Responsibility* (San Francisco: Ignatius Press, 1993), 182.

18. Maynard, *Josephine Bakhita*, 29.

19. Quotations in this paragraph are from Briere and Elliott, "Immediate and Long-Term Impacts of Child Sexual Abuse," 54–69.

20. Maynard, *Josephine Bakhita*, 37.

21. Ibid., 43.

22. Ibid., 48.

23. Ibid., 49.

24. Benedict XVI, *Spe Salvi*, 3.

25. Maynard, *Josephine Bakhita*, 50.

26. Benedict XVI, *Spe Salvi*, 3.

27. Ibid.

28. Ibid.

29. Maynard, *Josephine Bakhita*, 54.

30. Ibid., 55.

31. "Josephine Bakhita," www.vatican.va/news_services /liturgy/saints/ns_lit_doc_20001001_giuseppina-bakhita _en.html.

32. Maynard, *Josephine Bakhita*, 68.

33. Conference given in Notre Dame de Paris for the Fourth Sunday of Lent, 30 March 2003, by Cardinal Poupard, President of the Vatican Pontifical Council for Culture, www.vigilsd.org /adoc02_03.htm.

34. John Paul II, "Eucharistic Concelebration in Honor of Blessed Josephine Bakhita," www.vatican.va/holy_father /john_paul_ii/homilies/1993/documents/hf_jp-ii_hom _19930210_khartoum_en.html.

35. *The New Raccolta*, 60.

Chapter 2: The Love That Shelters

1. *CCC*, 477, 478.

2. Benedict XVI, *Spe Salvi*, 50.

3. Bessel A. van der Kolk et al., "A General Approach to Treatment of Posttraumatic Stress Disorder," in *Traumatic Stress: The Effects of Overwhelming Experience on Mind, Body, and Society*, ed. van der Kolk, MacFarlane, and Weiseath (New York: Guilford Press, 1996, 2007), 419–20, 429.

4. E-mail to author, June 14, 2011.

5. José Granados, "Through Mary's Memory to Jesus' Mystery," *Communio* 33 (Spring 2006): 24.

6. Joseph Cardinal Ratzinger, *Seek That Which Is Above* (San Francisco: Ignatius Press, 2007), 13, 14–15.

7. "Josephine Bakhita," www.vatican.va/news_services /liturgy/saints/ns_lit_doc_20001001_giuseppina-bakhita _en.html.

8. C. S. Lewis, *Surprised by Joy: The Shape of My Early Life* (Orlando, FL: Houghton Mifflin Harcourt, 1995), 14.

9. A helpful article on the meaning of Matthew 27:46 is Thomas Joseph White, O.P.'s "Jesus' Cry on the Cross and His Beatific Vision," *Nova et Vetera* #5, no. 3, English Edition (2007): 555–582.

10. John Henry Newman, Sermon 5, www.newmanreader .org/works/parochial/volume2/sermon5.html.

11. John Henry Newman, Sermon 11, www.newmanreader .org/works/parochial/volume4/sermon11.html.

12. John Henry Newman, Sermon 22, www.newmanreader .org/works/parochial/volume5/sermon22.html.

Chapter 3: The Love That Suffers

1. John Paul II, *Salvifici Doloris*, 24.

2. I am speaking here of the controversy over the technique known broadly as "Inner Healing," in which the therapist leads the trauma victim through a guided visualization of a traumatic memory. The victim is then instructed to bring Jesus into the memory—visualizing him as being a witness to the trauma, asking him questions, and listening for his "answers." There has been no formal research on the approach, but some who are familiar with it have asserted that it may do more harm than help.

3. Meriol Trevor, *Pope John* (Herefordshire, UK: Gracewing, 2000), 44.

4. *The Acts of the Christian Martyrs*, trans. Herbert Musurillo (Oxford: Oxford University Press, 2000), www.pbs.org/wgbh /pages/frontline/shows/religion/maps/primary/perpetua. html.

5. Terry Nelson, "Que Muero Porque No Muero," October 11, 2006, http://abbey-roads.blogspot.com/2006/10/que-muero -porque-no-muero.html.

6. Sr. Saint Michael, *Portrait of St. Gemma* (New York: P.J. Kennedy & Sons, 1949), 7.

7. Ibid., 44–45.

8. Emile Bougaud, *The Life of St. Margaret Mary Alacoque*, trans. a Visitandine of Maryland (Rockford, IL: TAN Books, 1990), 169. St. Margaret Mary Alacoque's recollection of the words of Jesus falls under the category of officially recognized private revelation. The Catechism states, "Throughout the ages, there have been so-called 'private' revelations, some of which have been recognized by the authority of the Church. They do not belong, however, to the deposit of faith. It is not their role to improve or complete Christ's definitive Revelation, but to help live more fully by it in a certain period of history" (*CCC* 67). In other words, while the faithful are not bound to believe them, officially recognized private revelations may help them better live the Christian life.

9. John Paul II, Message for the 13th World Communications Day: "Social Communications for the Development of the Child," May 27, 1979.

10. Briere and Elliott, "Immediate and Long-Term Impacts of Child Sexual Abuse."

11. Peter F. Ryan, S.J., "How to Discern the Elements of Your Personal Vocation," *Fellowship of Catholic Scholars Quarterly* 30, no. 1 (Summer 2007): 13. www.catholicscholars.org/publications/quarterly/v30n2sum2007.pdf.

12. Benedict XVI, *Spe Salvi*, 39.

Chapter 4: The Love That Transforms

1. Second Vatican Council, *Gaudium et Spes*, 14 §1.

2. Colin O'Brien, "Dualism, Zombies, and Persistently Conscious Heads," June 7, 2009, http://sparrowfallen.blogspot.com/2008/06/dualism-zombies-and-persistently.html.

3. See St. Thomas Aquinas, *Summa Theologiae* III (supplement), q. 85, a. 1.

4. O'Brien, "Dualism."

5. Ibid.

6. See St. Thomas Aquinas, *Summa Theologiae* I–II, q. 4, a. 5.

7. See Second Vatican Council, *Gaudium et Spes*, 11.

8. Guy Gaucher, *The Passion of Thérèse of Lisieux* (New York: Crossroad, 2006), 172.

9. St. Thérèse of Lisieux, *The Story of a Soul*, trans. John Clarke (Washington, DC: ICS Publications, 1976), 13, italics in original.
Thérèse is referring to Psalm 89:2: "I will sing of the mercies of the Lord for ever."

10. Ibid., 16–17.

11. Ibid., 266.

12. Gaucher, *Passion*, 178.

13. St. Thérèse, *Story*, 27.

14. Ibid., 30.

15. Ibid., 33.

16. Ibid., 34.

17. Gaucher, *Passion*, 178.

18. St. Thérèse, *Story*, 97.

19. Ibid., 98.

20. Ibid., 98, 99.

21. Ibid., 99.

22. St. Thérèse of Lisieux, quoted in Bishop A.A. Noser, *Joy in Suffering* (Rockford, IL: TAN Books, 2005), 36.

23. Gaucher, *Passion*, 174.

24. Ibid., 135.

25. Ibid., 180.

26. Ibid., 183.

27. Benedict XVI, General Audience, April 6, 2011, http://
www.vatican.va/holy_father/benedict_xvi/audiences/2011
/documents/hf_ben-xvi_aud_20110406_en.html.

Chapter 5: The Love That Liberates

1. For more on what this verse means in the life of the
Church, including how "God permits evil in order to draw forth
some greater good," see *CCC*, 412.

2. Mark Shea, "And Forgive Us Our Trespasses," http://www
.mark-shea.com/ofVIII.html.

3. The website for Stop It Now! (www.stopitnow.com), listed
in the resource guide on page 204, has advice for those facing
the responsibility of reporting an abuser.

4. See *Mystici Corporis Christi*, 18, where Pius XII speaks of
the sacraments as providing for the "life, health, and growth" of
the Mystical Body. Prayer is an essential part of our sacramental
life.

5. Alexander Gits, S.J., *A Modern Virgin Martyr: St. Maria
Goretti* (London: Catholic Truth Society, 1958), www.catholic
pamphlets.net/pamphlets/A%20Modern%20Virgin%20Martyr-
St%20Maria%20Goretti.pdf.

6. "Josephine Bakhita," www.vatican.va/news_services
/liturgy/saints/ns_lit_doc_20001001_giuseppina-bakhita
_en.html.

7. G. K. Chesterton, "A Piece of Chalk," www.gkc.org.uk
/gkc/books/chalk.html.

8. Leo XIII, *Mirae Caritatis*, 8.

9. Ibid., 6.

10. In calling lust for what it is—"dehumanizing" and "evil"—it's important to bear in mind that not all sexual attraction is lust. The Catechism states that, insofar as the passions arise from the senses rather than the mind, "there is neither moral good nor evil [in them]. But insofar as they engage reason and will, there is moral good or evil in them" (CCC 1773). In other words, it is not our passions themselves, but what we do with them that determines whether they lead us toward God or away from him. In the case of sexual attraction, sin enters in when a person fosters sexual desire that is detached from marital love and openness to children (see CCC 2351).

11. Salesian Proper for January 22, memorial for Laura Vicuña.

12. "Hundred Years Ago Blessed Laura Vicuna Died for Love," Fides News Service, January 21, 2004, www.fides.org /eng/news/2004/0401/21_1558.html.

13. John Cussen, "La Beata Laura Vicuña: The Nun's Version, Corrective of García Márquez's," *Religion and the Arts* 11 (2007): 402.

Chapter 6: The Love That Grows Deeper

1. The quotations in this paragraph are all from Robert Coles, *Dorothy Day: A Radical Devotion* (Cambridge, MA: Da Capo Press, 1987), 37.

2. Coles, *Dorothy Day: A Radical Devotion*, 37.

3. Ibid., 38.

4. For advice on finding a good spiritual director, see Resources, pages 195–199.

5. John C. Edwards, S.J., *Ways of Forgiveness* (Oxford, England: Family Publications, 1996), 10, 11.

6. Ibid., 11.

7. All quotations in this paragraph are from Sarah Dickerson, unpublished notes for "Wounded Sexuality Talk," 2011.

8. Dickerson, "Wounded Sexuality Talk."

9. Dorothy Day, *The Long Loneliness* (New York: HarperOne, 1981 [originally published 1952]), 60.

10. Ibid., 60.

11. Ibid., 27.

12. Ibid., 28.

13. For the text of the *Te Deum*, see Reader's Guide, pages 188–189.

14. Day, *Long Loneliness*, 35.

15. Dorothy Day, "Random Reflections," *Catholic Worker*, June 1944, 1, 2. www.catholicworker.org/dorothyday/daytext .cfm?TextID=401.

16. Day, *Long Loneliness*, 42.

17. Dorothy Day, *From Union Square to Rome*, chapter 4, www .catholicworker.org/dorothyday/Reprint2.cfm?TextID=204.

18. Day, *Long Loneliness*, 52.

19. Ibid., 60.

20. Ibid.

21. Stephen J. Krupa, "Celebrating Dorothy Day," *America*, August 27, 2001, www.americamagazine.org/content/article .cfm?article_id=1140.

22. Day, *Long Loneliness*, 116.

23. Ibid., 139.

24. Ibid., 120.

25. Ibid.

26. Ibid., 136.

27. Dan Lynch, "Dorothy Day's Pro-Life Memories," Catholic Exchange.com, September 24, 2002, republished by Catholic Education Resource Center, www.catholiceducation.org /articles/abortion/ab0063.html.

28. Day, *Long Loneliness*, 141.

29. Coles, *Dorothy Day: A Radical Devotion*, 62.

30. Day, *Long Loneliness*, 148.

31. Day, *From Union Square to Rome*, chapter 13.

32. Day, *Long Loneliness*, 166.

33. Dorothy Day, "On Pilgrimage—March 1966," *The Catholic Worker*, March 1966, www.catholicworker.org/dorothyday /daytext.cfm?TextID=249.

34. Day, *Long Loneliness*, 236.

35. Rita Simmonds and Webster Bull, "You Are Still My Mother," May 1, 2011, www.traces-cl.com/2011/05/youare still.html.

36. David Scott, *Praying in the Presence of Our Lord with Dorothy Day* (Huntington, IN: Our Sunday Visitor, 2002), 34.

37. Jim Forest, "Remembering Dorothy Day," www.jimand nancyforest.com/2005/01/09/remembering.

38. Simmonds and Bull, "You Are Still My Mother."

39. Day, *Long Loneliness*, 35.

40. Dorothy Day, "Random Reflections," *The Catholic Worker*, June 1944, www.catholicworker.org/dorothyday/Reprint2 .cfm?TextID=401.

41. Dorothy even wrote a book about the Little Flower: *Therese: A Life of Therese of Lisieux* (Springfield, IL: Templegate Publishers, 1960).

42. John Paul II, *Dives in Misericordia*, 13.

Chapter 7: The Love That Radiates

1. See the thirteenth-century classic *The Golden Legend*, compiled by James de Voragine.

2. See *Golden Legend*. I have modernized the language of William Caxton's 1483 translation.

3. Bernard of Clairvaux, *Commentary on the Song of Songs*, Sermon 20, www.archive.org/stream/St.BernardOn TheSongOfSongs/StBernardOnTheSongOfSongsall_djvu.txt.

4. Bernard of Clairvaux, *Commentary on the Song of Songs*, Sermon 26.

5. Ibid.

6. All quotations in this paragraph are from Bernard of Clairvaux, *Commentary on the Song of Songs*, Sermon 26.

7. Bernard of Clairvaux, *Commentary on the Song of Songs*, Sermon 26.

8. Ibid.

9. The English translation given of this phrase is that of Benedict XVI in *Spe Salvi*, 39. For more on this phrase and the Church's teachings on the redemptive value of human suffering, see chapter 3.

10. Bernard of Clairvaux, *Commentary on the Song of Songs*, Sermon 26.

11. For a comprehensive account of the biblical foundations of Catholic rituals and traditions, see Scott Hahn's *The Lamb's Supper: The Mass as Heaven on Earth* (New York: Doubleday, 1999).

12. Day, *Long Loneliness*, 59.

13. All biographical information on Kolbe in this chapter is taken from "St. Maximilian Kolbe," www.catholic-pages.com /saints/st_maximilian.asp.

14. G. K. Chesterton, "A Piece of Chalk," www.gkc.org.uk /gkc/books/chalk.html.

15. See Further Reading for recommendations of St. Maximilian's writings.

16. See *CCC*, 721–725.

Chapter 8: The Love That Heals

1. Michail Ford, O.P., "To Serve and Protect," *Vision* magazine (2009), www.digitalvocationguide.org/vision/2009/?pg=41.

2. Kenelm Foster, *The Life of Saint Thomas Aquinas: Biographical Documents* (London: Longmans, Green, 1959), 30.

3. St. Thomas Aquinas, *Summa Theologiae* III, q. 61, a. 1.

4. Dominican Fathers, "The Cord of St. Thomas," *The Rosary* (June 1896): 642.

5. Aquinas, *Summa Theologiae* II–II, q. 151, a. 2.

6. St. Thomas Aquinas, "The Catechetical Instructions of St. Thomas Aquinas," trans. Rev. Joseph B. Collins, www .documentacatholicaomnia.eu/03d/1225-1274,_Thomas _Aquinas,_Catechismus,_EN.pdf.

7. Terry Nelson, "Saints Like Us," June 11, 2001, http:// abbey-roads.blogspot.com/2011/06/saints-like-us.html.

8. "Bl. Albertina Berkenbrock (1919–1931)," www.vatican .va/news_services/liturgy/saints/ns_lit_doc_20071020 _berkenbrock_en.html.

9. Very little information on Blessed Karolina Kózka is available in English. For most of the information in this chapter, I am indebted to Maria Krzemińska, who provided a translation

of a Polish-language article by Ryszarda Kurka, www.pz.lap
.pl / ?id=news&pokaz=newsa&news_id=93.

Other information is drawn from a book-length Polish-
language biography of the saint by Bishop P. Bednarc-
zyk, excerpts of which were likewise translated for me by
Krzemińska.

10. Translation by Maria Krzemińska.

11. Quoted in the Ryszarda Kurka article, translated by
Maria Krzemińska.

12. For the entire poem, see Reader's Guide, pages 189–190.

13. Adapted from M. Gavin, S.J., *The Sacrifice of the Mass*
(London: Burns & Oates, 1903), chapter 13, www.the-latinmass
.com / id213.html.

14. Drusilla Barron, "Hell Doesn't Own Me," July 21, 2011,
http:/ / heirsinhope.blogspot.com / 2011 / 07 / experiment-7-hell
-doesnt-own-me.html.

15. Barron, "Hell Doesn't Own Me."

16. Dante Alighieri, *Paradiso*, Canto III, line 85.

Resources

1. United States Conference of Catholic Bishops, "Charter
for the Protection of Children and Young People," Article 1,
www.usccb.org / issues-and-action / child-and-youth-protection
/ upload / Charter-for-the-Protection-of-Children-and-Young
-People-revised-2011.pdf.

2. Benedict XVI, "Address to the Community of the Pontifical
Theological Faculty 'Teresianum,'" May 19, 2011, http:/ / www
.vatican.va / holy_father / benedict_xvi / speeches / 2011 / may
/ documents / hf_ben-xvi_spe_20110519_teresianum_en.html.

3. See C. Coppens, "Spiritual Direction," in *The Catholic
Encyclopedia* (New York: Robert Appleton Company, 1909), www
.newadvent.org / cathen / 05024a.htm.

4. Benedict XVI, General Audience, September 16, 2009.

5. Ibid.

D awn Eden is the bestselling author of *The Thrill of the Chaste: Finding Fulfillment While Keeping Your Clothes On*, which is in its eleventh printing and has been translated into Spanish, Polish, and Chinese. Born into a Jewish family in New York City, she lost her faith as a teenager and became an agnostic. During her twenties, in the 1990s, she worked as a rock journalist, interviewing bands for magazines and appearing as a music expert on TV's FX Network. Eden went on to work for several New York City newspapers, including the *New York Post* and the *Daily News*.

At age thirty-one, she experienced a dramatic conversion to Christianity that eventually led her to enter the Catholic Church. Now living in Washington, DC, Eden received a master's degree in theology from the Dominican House of Studies in 2010 and is studying toward a doctorate. She has spoken about chastity and conversion to thousands of college students and young adults throughout North America and abroad.

Founded in 1865, Ave Maria Press,
a ministry of the Congregation of
Holy Cross, is a Catholic publishing
company that serves the spiritual and
formative needs of the Church and its
schools, institutions, and ministers;
Christian individuals and families; and
others seeking spiritual nourishment.

For a complete listing of titles from

Ave Maria Press

Sorin Books

Forest of Peace

Christian Classics

visit www.avemariapress.com

ave maria press® / Notre Dame, IN 46556
A Ministry of the United States Province of Holy Cross